"Rick" Ames volunteered to spy for the KGB inside his own agency. He spoke Russian, knew the KGB extremely well, and had access to the names of Soviet spies risking their lives to secretly work for the United States. And Ames betrayed them all.

The Cold War officially ended at Christmastime 1991. The Soviet Union disbanded, leaving in its place America's new rival, the Russian Federation. Russia's new foreign spy service, replacing the KGB, was the SVR, the Foreign Intelligence Service. Even though the Cold War was declared over, the spying between Washington and Moscow never stopped—and, many experts say, neither did the Cold War.

CHAPTER I

The very worst day of Special Agent Leslie G. "Les" Wiser's long career in the FBI came on a warm, cloudy Thursday in September 1993.

Wiser, a veteran spy hunter, was on the biggest case of his life. His target was Aldrich Ames, a highly trained CIA officer. The FBI suspected Ames, who went by Rick, of selling some of America's deepest secrets to Russian spies. Ames, the bureau believed, had told the KGB, the Soviet Union's notorious spy service, the names of Soviet bloc—communist country—spies secretly working for the United States. Those cold-blooded betrayals led to the executions of at least ten foreign agents who had helped the United States and its allies.

The FBI code-named the Ames investigation NIGHT-MOVER.

Wiser's job was to collect enough evidence against Ames to arrest him. If he succeeded, his bosses would hail him a hero. If he failed, Wiser would go down in FBI lore as the agent who let a killer spy get away. So far, he and his Washington-based team had collected many clues that implicated Ames. But they had yet to collect any hard evidence that Ames was spying for Russia.

That Thursday, the ninth day of September, had started with such great promise. FBI agents on Wiser's team had intercepted a curious phone call between Ames and his wife, Rosario, who asked him to pick up their young son, Paul, at preschool that day. Ames agreed to, but said he would have to take an early-morning drive beforehand.

"What for?" Rosario asked.

"I have that, uh, errand I have to do," he said.

"Oh, one of those?"

"Yes," he said.

Wiser and his team knew something was up. They thought their target might try to make contact with Russia's new foreign spy service, the SVR. They hoped to

Spies with Russia's foreign intelligence service, the SVR, communicated with him through messages like these, which were loaded into dead drops.

catch Ames in the act of placing a note in a secret spot where the Russians could later pick it up. They suspected that Ames used such spots, called dead drops, to avoid being caught. On this day, however, agents hoped they might even catch Ames in a rendezvous with an SVR officer.

The NIGHTMOVER team set up a plan.

Wiser ordered the FBI's Special Surveillance Group—known as the Gs—to meet near Ames's home before 6 A.M. that Thursday. He wanted the Gs to tail Ames when he left his expensive home in Arlington, Virginia. They would have to be extremely careful not to let Ames know they were following him. After all, Ames was a professionally trained spy. He would know how surveillance teams worked.

The Gs made an unfortunate mistake that morning. They met in a parking lot near Ames's house. They were still there just before sunup, when Ames slipped behind the wheel of his shiny red Jaguar XJ6 and drove away. By the time the Gs got organized and reached Ames's home, their target had already returned from his "errand." They spotted his Jaguar in the driveway.

Agents checked an FBI video camera hidden on a telephone pole in front of Ames's house. Their subject had pulled away at 6:03 A.M. and returned twenty minutes later.

Wiser's team had no clue where Ames had gone.

If this had been a game, the score would have been NIGHTMOVER 1, FBI 0. But this was no game. Human lives and America's security were at stake.

That afternoon, one of the top officials in the FBI summoned Wiser to his office and chewed him out. It certainly wasn't Wiser's fault that the Gs had failed to show up in time to see Ames leave. But the blame landed on his shoulders because he was managing the case. Wiser didn't explain how the mistake had occurred. But he did say, very politely, that the NIGHTMOVER team still had

4

a chance to catch Ames in the act of spying for the Russians. The day, he said, wasn't over.

"And then," as Wiser explained with a laugh years later, "it got worse."

He ordered the Gs to set up their cars on both sides of a main road outside CIA headquarters. The agency's massive, highly secure compound overlooked the Potomac River in McLean, Virginia, a short drive from Washington, D.C. Wiser knew Ames planned to leave work that afternoon to take his wife and son to parents' night at Paul's preschool. He asked the Gs to put eyes on Ames as he drove home, hoping they might catch him in a rendezvous with one of his Russian spy pals.

A little after 4 P.M., the surveillance team spotted Ames's Jaguar leaving the CIA compound. They moved into traffic to follow. But the Jaguar, with a top speed of 140 miles per hour, suddenly took off like a frightened cat. The Gs couldn't follow Ames at such a breakneck speed because he would surely see them giving chase. Making matters worse, the tracking beacon that the FBI had secretly installed in Ames's Jag seven weeks earlier wasn't performing well—this was long before the FBI used GPS. Their tracking device, which operated by radio signal, was supposed to help them follow Ames's car. When the FBI chase car drew close to the Jaguar, the Gs could hear loud beeps. When the target car was farther away, the beeps grew faint. What the Gs now heard from Ames's car was no beeping at all. He and his Jag were gone.

Wiser heard the frustrating news by FBI radio. But he knew his team had another chance to spot Ames driving home from work. An FBI surveillance plane, one of the bureau's eyes in the sky, had been scheduled to take off from a nearby airport to track Ames's movements. But Wiser now heard more bad news. The pilot, for whatever reason, had failed to take off in time to observe the Jaguar. Ames had vanished again.

NIGHTMOVER 2, FBI 0.

"I was pretty frustrated," Wiser later explained. He and the rest of the NIGHTMOVER team were disappointed. Losing Ames twice in a single day was bad enough, but not knowing where he was going, or what he would do, made them feel worse.

As it happened, Rick Ames had been very, very busy.

Before sunup, he had made his way to Rock Creek Park on the north end of Washington. There, he placed a package for the Russians in a dead drop beneath a footbridge. After work that afternoon, Ames had driven to a wealthy neighborhood near the Russian Embassy. There, he stepped out of his Jaguar and drew a chalk line on a bright U.S. Postal Service mailbox. This mark let the Russians know he had left them a message at the bridge.

Wiser put the Gs on the street again that night to tail Ames. At about 7 P.M., they spotted their target and his family. Rick was at the wheel of the Jag. Rosario sat next to him, and four-year-old Paul was in the back seat. The Gs folded into the traffic behind him, following at a safe distance. They watched as the Jaguar parked at Paul's preschool in Alexandria, Virginia, and the Ames family walked inside. About an hour later, the Ameses climbed back into their car. Again, the Gs folded themselves into traffic. They expected to follow the family straight to their home.

An FBI surveillance plane, circling above, spotted the Jaguar speeding onto a bridge over the Potomac River. Wiser, listening to his radio, heard a voice crackle to life.

"He's going into the city!"

Agents tailed Ames into northwest Washington, D.C., and to a tree-lined neighborhood full of stately homes. There, he made an abrupt turn onto a quiet cul-de-sac called Garfield Terrace.

Ames pulled the Jaguar very slowly past a bright blue

mailbox. Then he turned the car around and headed home. Agents sensed that Ames was on a mission, but they didn't know the nature of that mission. Ames, they would later learn, was looking for a signal from his Russian pals.

The directors of the FBI and CIA were not pleased to hear that Wiser's team had blown two good chances to follow Ames on that miserable Thursday, and their moods didn't improve just because the Gs managed to tail Ames on the way home from Paul's school. After all, that trip had not led to any solid evidence.

Wiser was upset by the day's many disappointments. But he knew it hadn't been a complete failure. Rick Ames's movements—getting up much earlier than normal for a short trip in his car, gunning into traffic from the CIA exit road, taking a mysterious after-dark trip into D.C.—all served as clues.

He was acting just like a spy.

CHAPTER 2

Very few intelligence officers betray their countries. But counterspies such as Les Wiser Jr. know that when they do, they always have their reasons. Some switch loyalties because they hate their government. Others spy against their countries only after a foreign intelligence service blackmails them. Still others do it to boost their own egos. A few become traitors just for the thrill of it. But for most spies who switch teams, it's all about the money.

Exhibit A: Rick Ames.

In 1984, nine years before the FBI began to investigate Ames, he fell into financial trouble. He was married to one woman, former CIA officer Nancy Jane Segebarth, but dating another. His mistress, Rosario, whom he supported financially and hoped to marry, was burning through his money like wildfire. She ran up phone bills of $400 a month just to call her mother, who lived in South America. Meanwhile, Ames was fighting an expensive divorce battle. He would later have to pay his former wife $33,500 of the couple's combined debts, plus $300 a month in other support.

Ames was so worried about money that he later said he had fantasized about robbing a bank. But just before Thanksgiving 1984, he came up with another plan: He would smuggle highly guarded files out of the CIA and sell them to the Soviet intelligence service, the KGB. In many ways, this plan was *more* dangerous than robbing a bank. This kind of spy work could be deadly, and if he were caught, he would be tried for espionage. Wisely, he didn't share his idea with anyone—not even Rosario.

In February 1985, something mysterious happened while Ames was on official CIA business in London. There, as he later told author Pete Earley, he joined a group of other CIA officers in a pub. One of them described herself as a "practicing witch" and said she possessed a special power: She could tell when someone was a traitor. Ames, who was giving serious thought to selling out his country to the KGB, nearly laughed in her face.

"Well," he told her, "maybe you will have a chance to prove your powers someday."

Back in Washington, the CIA granted Ames permission to meet with Sergei Chuvakhin, a Soviet diplomat. Chuvakhin was an expert on nuclear arms control. The CIA hoped Ames could recruit him as a secret agent who could give the United States insights on the Soviet Union's nuclear capabilities. But Ames came up with a more sinister plan.

He set up a lunch date with Chuvakhin for April 16, 1985. He spent part of that day at CIA headquarters, typing out a treasonous letter. His words would change the course of his life. He addressed his note to the top KGB officer in Washington, known as the *rezident*. Ames gave his true name, explaining that he was branch chief of the CIA's Soviet counterintelligence division.

"I need $50,000," he wrote, "and in exchange for the money, here is information about three agents we are developing in the Soviet Union right now." These words let the KGB know that the CIA was about to recruit Soviet spies right under its nose.

Ames named the three spies and then tucked his note into a blank envelope. He carried it with him to the Mayflower Hotel, where he arrived a half hour early. Ames, who often drank too much, was so nervous that he gulped down three double vodkas to calm down. But Chuvakhin failed to show up for their meeting.

Frustrated and a little drunk, Ames got up from his seat and stalked a few blocks to the Soviet embassy. In the lobby, he walked straight to a clerk behind a glass window. There he asked to speak to Chuvakhin. The clerk picked up the phone, spoke a few words, and told Ames that Mr. Chuvakhin would be right down. Ames walked to a corner of the lobby and waited.

A moment later, before Chuvakhin arrived, Ames marched back to the window and slipped his envelope through to the receptionist. The clerk saw the name of the KGB *rezident* scribbled on the outside and nervously placed it out of sight. When Chuvakhin arrived in the lobby, Ames told him they must reschedule their lunch.

"I'll call you in a few weeks," Ames said.

"I'll be busy," Chuvakhin replied.

"We'll see," Ames said.

He was quite certain the KGB would ask Chuvakhin to reconnect with him because he had just volunteered to spy for the Soviets. Ames's betrayal was clever: The CIA would let him meet with Chuvakhin in the hope that he could recruit the Soviet official as a spy for the United States. But instead, Ames hoped to secretly work for the KGB.

Sure enough, Chuvakhin met Ames a month later in the lobby of the Soviet embassy. The diplomat guided him to a large conference room with no windows and opened the door for Ames, who walked inside. Chuvakhin remained outside.

Moments later, a tall, dark-haired man walked in and shook Ames's hand. His name was Colonel Victor Cherkashin. He was the top KGB counterintelligence officer at the embassy. Ordinarily, the colonel's job was to protect the embassy and its employees from U.S. spies like Ames. But Ames's letter had changed things.

The moment they shook hands, Ames and the KGB man became business associates. The colonel pulled a letter out of a pocket and handed it to Ames. He didn't say anything, just gestured with his hands for the CIA man to read it.

Ames looked the letter over. The KGB's message was clear: They were pleased to accept his offer and would pay him the $50,000. The letter also said that even though

Chuvakhin was not a KGB officer, he would serve as a messenger between Ames and the KGB. Ames stood and jotted a note on the back of the letter: "Okay, thank you very much."

In the lingo of professional spies, Rick Ames had just become a "walk-in"—an agent who volunteers to spy for another nation. Only much later did the enormity of what he had just done begin to frighten him. He had crossed a line, and there was no going back.

One day not long after, Ames met Chuvakhin for lunch at Joe and Mo's, a steakhouse in Washington. They discussed arms control and other matters. As their meal came to an end, the two men stood up to leave. Just then, Chuvakhin remembered something.

"Oh," he said, handing a bag to Ames. "Here are some press releases that I think you will find interesting."

Ames thanked him, walked out of the restaurant, and made his way to his car. He drove out of town and onto the George Washington Memorial Parkway, with its sweeping views of the Potomac River. He stopped the car at a scenic overlook and reached into the bag. Inside was a package wrapped in brown paper. Ames tore open a corner. Inside was a stack of five hundred $100 bills—$50,000.

The money was proof that Ames was a criminal working for America's most dangerous enemy. A mole inside the CIA. A traitor to the United States.

As Special Agent Wiser would explain many years later, Ames served the KGB as an "agent in place." That was a major prize for the Soviet intelligence service. Ames's job at the CIA—chief of a Soviet counterintelligence branch—gave him information about Soviets secretly working for the United States.

Ames felt terrified and exhilarated. That night, he hid the brick of cash in his closet. For the next several weeks, he moved through his days in a dreamlike state of shock.

On May 18, 1985, Ames deposited $9,000 of the KGB's cash into his checking account. He kept Rosario in the dark about the money. (Later he would invent a cover story, telling her it was from a college buddy who owed him a favor.)

Two days later, the FBI arrested John A. Walker Jr., a former Navy chief warrant officer, in a Maryland motel room less than twenty miles from Ames's apartment. Walker had been spying for the KGB since 1967, selling roughly a thousand U.S. military files to the Soviets. One document among them posed extremely grave danger to the United States. It identified all of America's missile targets inside the Soviet Union. These were the places America would bomb if war broke out between the United States and the USSR. This information was valuable to the Soviets because it allowed them to prepare for the attack. For his crimes, Walker faced life in prison.

Walker's arrest scared Ames. He had never heard of Walker, but the former Navy man's fate served as a reminder of the risks he too now faced. Yet Ames did not stop spying for the Soviets. Far from it, in fact.

His betrayals were only beginning.

CHAPTER 3

Inside the CIA, the first signs of trouble came in the fall of 1985.

Officers heard ominous reports about the arrests of Soviet agents who'd secretly worked for America. The KGB had lured Valery Martynov, one of its officers, back to Moscow. The security service also followed Leonid G. Poleshchuk, to a dead drop in Moscow and arrested him. And they dragged a Soviet military intelligence officer, Lieutenant Colonel Gennady Smetanin, and his wife, Svetlana, off a train in Moscow. All had supplied the United States with information.

One after another, the CIA lost contact with secret agents who were doing courageous work for America. By the end of 1986, the agency had lost all its assets from the Soviet Union—roughly two dozen simply vanished. Over the next few years, the agency would learn that the KGB had rounded them all up. The lucky ones were imprisoned. Ten, found guilty of treason against the Soviet Union, were put to death.

In some cases, KGB executioners walked these Soviet spies down a hallway and forced them to their knees. The last sound they heard was a single bullet fired into the back of their skull. The victims were buried in unmarked graves so that their families would have no place to weep for them.

To the KGB, these spies were traitors who deserved to die. To the CIA and FBI, they were heroes who had risked their lives working for America.

The loss of these brave agents, as Les Wiser would observe more than forty years later, had grave consequences. The secrets they had shared had opened a window into the plans, intentions, and capabilities of America's most important enemy. "The losses were like the window was closed," he said, "and night's darkness rendered us nearly blind."

U.S. intelligence officials took the news very badly. CIA officers who had assisted the betrayed agents, and were supposed to keep them safe, had failed. Worse, these handlers didn't know what mistakes they might have made—or how to guard against them in the future.

Veteran CIA officer Sandy Grimes, who managed the branch that handled Poleshchuk's spy operations, later recalled the terrible day of October 2, 1985. Her boss motioned for her to sit down and then handed her an excerpt from an overseas cable. It was bad news. Two months earlier, according to a Soviet source, the KGB had arrested one of its own officers.

Grimes felt sick to her stomach. She knew it was Poleshchuk, and she felt sure he was going to die. Grimes had arranged for a CIA officer in Moscow to stash $20,000 in Soviet rubles inside a fake rock in Izmaylovsky Park. Poleshchuk had been nabbed by the KGB when he went to pick up his money. Grimes now second-guessed herself, wondering if she had made a mistake that would cost Poleshchuk his life.

The words of a fellow CIA officer now rang in Grimes's head. He had warned her not to run a dead-drop operation in Moscow. Too risky, he had said. Now she wondered if that officer, a smart spy handler who spoke Russian, might have been right. The officer who had given Grimes that advice was none other than Rick Ames.

Little did Grimes know that Ames, surrounded by co-workers who had trusted him for years, had betrayed Poleshchuk's name to the KGB. He had studied the agency's secret cable messages about Poleshchuk at CIA headquarters, then dropped the man's name—and those of other Soviet spies—right into the KGB's lap. It was like throwing meat to the lions.

Grimes had also worked with another of the spies who turned up missing: General Dimitri F. Polyakov, code-named TOPHAT. He was the crown jewel of the CIA's Soviet agents. His loss deeply saddened Grimes. She had first worked with Polyakov in 1967 as a fresh-out-of-college file clerk, one of the few jobs open to women in the agency back then. She typed and cataloged details from the secrets Polyakov shared with the CIA.

"He gave us tons of stuff," she later said. "After he became a general, he was a gold mine." Polyakov had served with distinction in the GRU, the spy wing of the Soviet military. But secretly, for eighteen years, he had spied for America. He handed the FBI and the CIA a vast collection of secret Soviet reports. He named Soviet spies at work all over the world. And he delivered Soviet strategies for nuclear, chemical, and biological warfare. Those files helped the United States prevent World War III.

Polyakov had not spied for money, Grimes later explained. He did it out of patriotic duty to the Soviet Union. The general believed the USSR had fallen into the hands of corrupt leaders who might drive his homeland into a nuclear war with the United States. But Polyakov felt the United States was too weak to win the Cold War, so he stepped in to help.

CIA officers who admired Polyakov's contribution to world peace had casually let him know that he was always welcome to defect to the United States. The agency uses a 1949 law known as PL-110—sort of a witness protection program for spies—to relocate them and secure their safety. But the proud general never took his American friends up on this.

"I was born a Russian, and I will die a Russian," he said. Polyakov wanted to retire in his homeland. But he knew that if he was exposed there as an American spy, he would be shot to death, and his corpse would be dropped into an unmarked grave.

Indeed, that was Polyakov's fate.

Years later, Grimes heard definitive news of the

general's death. "I couldn't catch my breath," she recalled. "I guess it was like a death in the family. . . . Everybody was feeling the same way. It was a terrible, terrible loss." Grimes and other CIA officers believed Polyakov and the agency's other dead sources deserved their best efforts to find out who had given up their names.

This was the genesis of the CIA probe that later grew into the Ames mole hunt.

CHAPTER 4

Rick Ames, having informed to the KGB about Polyakov and the others, had put an end to his money troubles. But a new problem emerged. He was rattled by fear. Ames knew that if the United States caught him spying for the KGB, life as he knew it was over. Punishment for the crime of espionage was a long prison term—in some cases, even death. So he came up with a devious plan to reduce his chances of being caught.

Ames's job as a counterspy supervisor gave him access to cable messages between headquarters and CIA officers in the field. This meant he knew about the Soviet bloc spies secretly working for the agency. They were among the CIA's most prized assets. They risked their lives to spy for America, and those who spied for money were paid well for their services. Many of them continued to work as Soviet intelligence officers while they spied for America, and Ames knew that as part of their work, one might learn that Ames was secretly working for the Soviets. The possibility that they might betray him to the CIA worried him sick.

So he decided to eliminate every one of them.

Ames's plan was to inform on those assets before they could inform on him. He knew that handing over their identities to the KGB meant prison for some and death for others. But the way he saw things, it was his life or theirs.

"Now that I was working for the KGB," Ames would tell an interviewer years later, "the people on my list could expect nothing less from me. It wasn't personal. It was how the game was played."

So in early 1985, Ames had begun a deadly game of treachery. At his desk on the fourth floor of the CIA's Original Headquarters Building, he reviewed what were then known as "restricted-handling" files. These were reports, memos, and overseas cables on all the Soviet agents working for the United States and its allies.

On June 13, 1985, Ames jotted a message to the KGB. He loaded that note and hundreds of pages of the CIA's deepest secrets into plastic bags. These he dropped into his briefcase, which he carried down to the lobby. Ames then walked through a security turnstile as easily as if he were making his way onto a subway platform. He headed for his car, which sat in the sprawling parking lot outside headquarters.

Ames had just smuggled out the biggest trove of CIA secrets in the agency's history. No security officer stopped him to look inside his briefcase. In past years, security officers had sometimes checked employees' bags on the way out, but the searches had caused bottlenecks and made employees late to get home, so the CIA had ended them.

It was lunchtime when Ames pulled out of CIA headquarters. America's newest turncoat drove toward his nation's capital on two highways named for patriots. He motored down George Washington Memorial Parkway, named for the first president, and crossed the Francis Scott Key Bridge, which honored the author of "The Star-Spangled Banner." Ames pulled his car into Washington's Georgetown neighborhood. He walked into Chadwicks, a restaurant known for its weekend champagne brunches. There, he met with Sergei Chuvakhin.

When their meal ended, Chuvakhin carried out a bag full of files that named twenty Soviet agents on the CIA payroll. The list included two KGB officers who worked in Washington's Soviet embassy, Lieutenant Colonel Valery Martynov and Major Sergei Motorin. Also named in the files was Adolf Tolkachev, an electronics engineer in Moscow who passed data on Soviet aircraft and missiles to the CIA. Tolkachev was such a valuable asset that a book later published about his life was titled *The Billion Dollar Spy*. Ames's bag of betrayals also included the name of the KGB's Colonel Vladimir Piguzov, who had helped the CIA by letting the agency know that one of its retired officers had sold secrets to the KGB.

The biggest name Chuvakhin carried away from Chadwicks that day was Polyakov, the general whose arrest would so upset Grimes and other CIA officers.

Throughout 1985 and into the next year, Ames would meet with Chuvakhin fourteen times. He passed bags full of files to the Soviet diplomat, who turned them over to the KGB. In turn, Chuvakhin handed Ames bags that the KGB had prepared for him. Each held bricks of cash ranging from $20,000 to $50,000.

The money allowed Ames to settle his divorce, stash a bundle in the bank, and spoil his new wife, Rosario. But on August 1, 1986, Ames confronted a new and potentially dangerous threat to his secret arrangement with the KGB.

On that day, the KGB's Colonel Vitaly Yurchenko walked into the U.S. embassy in Rome, Italy, and defected to the CIA. The colonel was a great prize for America. Just a few years earlier he had served in Washington, running Soviet spy operations against the United States. Now, like Ames, he had secretly switched teams.

Ames was among the first CIA officers to learn of Yurchenko's defection. He worried that Yurchenko might know he was the KGB's mole inside the CIA. This worry turned into panic when Ames's superiors assigned him to meet Yurchenko at Andrews Air Force Base, in Maryland just outside Washington, D.C. His assignment was to take Colonel Yurchenko to a safe house and interview him over many days. That process is called debriefing.

Ames feared that when he met Yurchenko, surrounded by other intelligence officers, Yurchenko might point at Ames and shout, "That man's a KGB spy!" But Ames had no way to get out of the meeting.

When Ames and his team of CIA officers met with Yurchenko, Ames calmed himself, as always, by smoking one cigarette after another. But if Yurchenko was aware of Ames's secret life, he didn't let on. The two men met from 9 A.M. to 1 P.M. on twenty different days that summer. They got along well; the colonel even scolded

Ames for his heavy smoking. CIA officers and FBI agents often joined them for the debriefings.

Yurchenko surprised his listeners by confessing that he had once headed a team of deep-cover spies at the Russian embassy in Washington. These "sleeper" spies were to be activated, possibly as saboteurs, in the event of war between the Soviet Union and the United States. Yurchenko also gave descriptions of two Americans secretly working for the KGB. One was Ronald Pelton, who worked for the National Security Agency (NSA). Pelton had told the KGB about Operation Ivy Bells, in which the NSA bugged the Soviet navy's undersea communications cables. Pelton was later found guilty of espionage and sent to prison for thirty years. The other American was former CIA officer Edward Lee Howard, who came under investigation by the FBI and fled to Moscow. He would die in a mysterious fall in 2002.

Ames took mounds of notes during the debriefings. Later, of course, he passed what he learned about Yurchenko to the KGB. He had now been spying for the Soviets for more than a year. His life as a KGB mole remained a secret.

At least for now.

CHAPTER 5

The CIA worked tirelessly to find out who, or what, had betrayed their Soviet agents. But the KGB worked just as hard to confuse the Americans and protect Rick Ames. The last thing the Soviet spy agency wanted was for the CIA to realize there was a mole inside its own headquarters. So the KGB waged a campaign of deception.

Soviet spies planted false information about how the USSR had identified its betrayers. CIA officials took the bait, blaming some of the losses on poor tradecraft by their own officers. In addition, the agency explored another theory, also planted by the KGB, that the CIA's off-site communications center had been compromised.

Sandy Grimes spent years trying to solve the mystery.

She had grown convinced that Ames was the mole not only because he had access to all the Soviet case files, but also because of something she first learned one day in 1989. That was when a friend, CIA officer Diana Worthen, popped into her office. Years later, Grimes would remember that Worthen closed the door, took a seat, and bared her soul.

CIA officer Diana Worthen first raised concerns about the sudden wealth of her friends Rick and Rosario Ames in 1989.

"I know this sounds terrible," Worthen told her, "and I feel like I'm being a real rat doing this. I mean, these people are two of my closest friends. But I think there is something you need to know about them."

Worthen then recounted for Grimes how Rick and Rosario had lived when they first moved in together in the early 1980s.

Their home was a modest rental apartment seven miles from CIA headquarters. They drove a beat-up Volvo. But somehow, after the couple married in August 1985 (less than two weeks after Ames's divorce from his first wife), the Rick and Rosario she knew had vanished. The couple had spent four years in Rome, where Ames had been posted, and returned in late 1989 as very different people. The new Rick and Rosario lived in a $540,000 home in a wealthy section of Arlington, Virginia. They drove brand-new cars. They even looked different.

The old Rick dressed in worn-out jackets and discount shoes; his fingernails were dirty, and his teeth yellowed by years of cigarette smoking. But now, Worthen reported, Rick paid more attention to his grooming. He wore hand-tailored Italian suits, $600 shoes, designer sunglasses, and a Rolex watch. His teeth, newly capped, were white as pearls.

Grimes recalled the old Rick, who was four years older than she was. They had come up through the ranks of the CIA at the same time. They had ridden to work in the same carpool, Grimes with her Ford Pinto, Ames with his filthy blue Volvo with a broken window. Ames had made members of the carpool crazy because he was always late. Still, she thought of Rick as smart, happy-go-lucky, and fun to be around. Back in those days, he didn't seem to care about how he looked. She recalled that his posture was terrible. He was always slouching.

Like Worthen, Grimes had seen the transformation. Ames now dressed like a movie star, held his shoulders back and his head high, and seemed to look much more confident. But it wasn't confidence, Grimes decided. It was something else. Rick Ames looked arrogant, like a rich landowner overseeing his plantation. His attitude seemed to be *I know better than you do.*

Counterintelligence supervisor Jeanne Vertefeuille, who had joined the CIA in 1954 and broken ground for all the agency's women, agreed with her friend and co-worker Sandy Grimes that Ames might be a mole. Inside the CIA, Ames had told co-workers that Rosario's family was loaded. He added that they had been generous to him, allowing him to live way beyond the means of his CIA paychecks. Vertefeuille wanted to learn whether Ames's story of family wealth was true or not. She dispatched a CIA officer to Bogotá, Colombia, the home of Rosario's family, to find out if they really were rich.

A local investigator poked around and found, sure enough, that Rosario's family was indeed wealthy.

They owned large tracts of land, ran an import-export business, and had invested in a chain of ice-cream stores. Only much later would the CIA learn that the investigator

Jeanne Vertefeuille, an expert in Soviet counterintelligence, served as a CIA officer from 1954 to 1992. She later worked as a contract analyst for the agency.

had done a poor job. Rosario's mom and dad were politically connected—they were even friends of Colombia's president—but they were not wealthy. But Vertefeuille knew none of this. Based on the faulty information, she and Grimes and others in CIA didn't zero in on Ames as the source of the leaks.

By spring 1991, Grimes was exhausted and ready to quit her job. She was forty-five years old and had given half her life to the CIA. The work had too often taken her away from her husband and two daughters.

Grimes told her boss, Paul Redmond, deputy chief of the CIA's Counterintelligence Center, that she was planning to quit the agency. A couple of days later, Redmond phoned her to ask a question: Would she be willing to team up with Jeanne Vertefeuille? He wanted them to take one last stab at solving the mystery of the 1985 losses.

"You've made me the only offer I could never refuse," she said.

CHAPTER 6

Paul Redmond assigned Grimes and Vertefeuille
to see if the KGB had a mole inside the CIA. They were
joined in that task by CIA security officer Dan Payne,
whose job was to safeguard the agency's employees and
their secrets. The FBI loaned two of its best spy hunters
to the team, Special Agent Jim Holt and Senior Analyst
Jim Milburn. Holt, much like Grimes, had a personal
stake in finding the mole. He had served as the handler
for Valery Martynov, the KGB officer executed in 1987.

Grimes and Vertefeuille still suspected that Rick
Ames might be their mole. However, they kept an open
mind as the group moved into a backroom office at CIA
headquarters. The team soon discovered that 160 CIA
employees had access to files on at least one of the Soviet

agents lost in 1985. Grimes and Vertefeuille pored over the list. They removed employees who clearly weren't likely to be traitors to their country. This was highly unscientific, of course, because even a traitor can pretend to be a patriot. The mole-hunting team, joined by three other CIA officers, cast votes on who they thought was most likely to be the mole. Their top choice was Rick Ames.

Grimes recalled that on her first day in the Counterintelligence Center, Ames had walked in to welcome her. She watched his expression as she told him that she and Vertefeuille had teamed up to take a new look at the disastrous losses of Soviet assets in 1985. Ames's face betrayed no emotion. Then, cocky as ever about his knowledge of the KGB, he offered her some pointers, Grimes recalled. Ames suggested that she look at differences between the assets and those now working for the CIA.

"If you need any help," Grimes recalled him saying, "just give me a call."

Yeah, right, she thought.

As part of their probe, everyone knowledgeable about these events in 1985 had to take a polygraph test. The purpose of these tests, often called "lie detectors," was to rule

Five CIA officers served on the Ames mole hunt team. They were, from left, Sandy Grimes, Paul Redmond, Jeanne Vertefeuille, Diana Worthen, and Dan Payne.

out those who were clearly not the mole. Grimes and Vertefeuille, both familiar with some of the dead assets, took their turns on "the box"—as polygraph machines were sometimes called—and both were ruled out as the mole.

Ames, secretly coached by the KGB, then took his turn on the box. He followed the Soviets' instructions: He got a good night's sleep before the test, stayed relaxed, and was chummy with the polygraph examiner. The operator hooked him up to the polygraph machine, which measures breathing, perspiration, blood pressure, and other signs of nervousness. Ames passed. But how can someone beat a lie detector?

Experts say the machine is only as good as the operator, who has to ask the right questions to know whether someone is being deceptive. In Ames's case, CIA investigators had not told the examiner all they knew about Ames. For instance, they did not share their suspicions about Ames's wealth. Had the operator asked questions about the source of his money, Ames might have reacted in a way that showed he was lying.

Later, Payne read the polygraph report. He learned that Ames had made an offhand remark to the polygraph examiner about Rosario's family rolling in dough. Ames had said he was just along for the ride. From then on, the CIA mole-hunt investigation went by the code name JOYRIDE.

After the lie-detector tests, Vertefeuille and Grimes set up an interview room and questioned roughly forty CIA employees. One by one, each took their turn answering questions written by Vertefeuille. One of them was, "Have you ever violated security inside the CIA?"

Ames's answer seemed rehearsed. He explained that the agency had once dressed him down for leaving open his office safe, which held top secret files. Neither Grimes nor Vertefeuille was surprised. They already knew about that incident. They also knew that Ames had once been given a stern talking-to about leaving a briefcase full of classified papers on a train in New York City.

Later in the interview, Ames threw Grimes and Vertefeuille a curve. Attempting to sound helpful, Ames explained that the safe he had left open in his office held files on some of the missing Soviet agents. This meant that anyone who had passed his safe could have secretly copied the papers and smuggled them to the KGB. Grimes and Vertefeuille saw right through Ames's story. They knew what he was doing.

Rick Ames was trying to build an alibi.

CHAPTER 7

The next step in proving Rick Ames was a KGB mole was a major project that Sandy Grimes launched in late 1991. She began to build a timeline of his life, CIA career, and possible crimes—a daily log of his activities that went back many years.

She obtained a mountain of records on her target, typing everything she could find on him into her computer. She charted all of his assignments, many of them in foreign nations, and all of his movements inside CIA headquarters.

For example, Ames, like all CIA employees, wore a blue badge that gave him access to the building. She documented the time and date of every time his badge passed in or out of headquarters. If Ames left the building—even for just a cigarette break—Grimes typed it into the timeline. She also entered data on Ames's official contacts with Soviets. This included his CIA-authorized meetings with Sergei Chuvakhin, whom he was supposed to be grooming for recruitment. Of course, unbeknownst to the CIA, Chuvakhin served as a middleman between Rick Ames and the KGB.

Grimes hoped her timeline, which eventually grew to more than five hundred pages, would show changes in Ames's behavior and spending habits.

Dan Payne got permission from the Department of Justice to ask Ames's banks for a secret look at his finances. He delivered what are called National Security Letters to Ames's banks. These letters required bank managers to secretly copy Ames's financial records and turn them over to the CIA. Under the law, these financial institutions could not tell Ames they had shared his bank information.

When an envelope full of records eventually came back, Payne got to work. He read reports on all of Ames's credit card charges, canceled checks, deposits, and withdrawals. Then he punched in the dates for every one of Ames's bank transactions. What he discovered blew his mind: Ames earned less than $70,000 a year at the CIA, yet he had somehow put $1.3 million in the bank over the last few years. Payne also learned that Ames often made cash deposits of $5,000 and $9,000, which was very suspicious. Criminals, he knew, often make large cash deposits. But the smart ones make them less than $10,000 because U.S. law requires Americans to report when they put that much cash in the bank. Ames's cash deposits looked more like those of a drug kingpin than of a public servant.

Payne punched all the deposits into his spreadsheet and, in the summer of 1992, handed a printout to Grimes at the desk next to him. Grimes added the data to her massive timeline. Soon, she made an eye-popping connection. Ames had met for lunch with Chuvakhin, the Soviet arms-control expert, in three CIA-authorized meetings in May and July 1985. This was about the time that the CIA's Soviet assets had begun to vanish. After each of these lunches, Ames had gone to the bank to make large cash deposits into his accounts—$9,000 . . . $5,000 . . . $8,500.

Grimes excitedly told the team her news. Then she hurried to the office of her boss, Paul Redmond.

"It doesn't take a rocket scientist to tell what's going on here," she told Redmond. "Rick is a Russian spy!" (For the record, Grimes used a salty adjective in front of the word "Russian.")

Redmond nodded. He too was convinced Ames was their mole.

It was at about this time, in the summer of 1992, that Rosario Ames learned the true source of her husband's money.

She found a typewritten note in one of Rick's wallets that was clearly in spy-like code. One line on the paper mentioned "the city where your mother-in-law lives." Furious, Rosario tore into her husband. She told him not to involve her family in his CIA work.

Rick Ames dismissed her concerns, telling her not to worry. But a few weeks later, he sat her down in a Vietnamese restaurant in Georgetown to confess. Ames admitted that his money had not come from an old college friend or any kind of investments.

"I'm working for the Russians," he said.

Rosario, horrified, scarcely knew what to do. She had no intention of going to the FBI. That, she knew, would ruin their very comfortable lives. But she did come up with a plan of action. From that day forward, she watched over Ames very carefully, grilling him about every illegal spy move he made. She wanted to make sure he didn't do anything stupid that would get them both caught.

The CIA could not arrest Ames, because the agency is not—despite what many people think—a law enforcement agency. When CIA officials discover serious criminal activity by their employees—especially spies in their ranks—they report them to the FBI.

The Ames mole-hunt team soon shared its findings with the FBI. Grimes and Vertefeuille were sorely disappointed when the bureau did not immediately move in to arrest Ames. In fact, the FBI didn't even open a criminal investigation of him, because they viewed Ames as just one of several potential double agents in the CIA.

The news left Grimes and others on the team shocked, sickened, and angry.

"We were totally convinced that Rick was our mole," she later said. Vertefeuille told her that Ames would simply retire from the CIA and move to Colombia with Rosario and their son. There, Vertefeuille feared, they would live like the rich and famous on what she called "Rick's blood money."

Then in 1993, the CIA benefited from a small miracle.

The agency got information from one of its assets—likely an SVR officer—that pointed them in the direction of Ames. The identity of that asset, and the information he provided, remains a closely guarded national secret. But this much is known: The CIA shared this information with the FBI in hopes that the bureau would change its mind and target Ames for criminal investigation.

They got their wish.

On May 12, 1993, Robert M. "Bear" Bryant, the special agent in charge of the FBI's Washington field office, opened a criminal investigation into Aldrich Hazen Ames for espionage.

CHAPTER 8

Spy hunters such as Les Wiser Jr. are a unique
breed.

To be a counterspy, you have to be equal parts cop,
bloodhound, national security scholar, magician, and
chess master. Spy cases sometimes take years to clear
up. The investigations are so secretive that only a small
number of agents are allowed to know about them. The
agents can't tell anyone about their cases. And when
they have a bad day at work, or a good one, they can't
even tell their spouses or their children. It's a thankless
job. But many who do it well say that a good spy hunt is
positively thrilling.

On the afternoon of May 24, 1993, Wiser's boss
summoned him to his eleventh-floor office in the FBI's

Washington Metropolitan Field Office. The office occupied a building in a gritty part of town known as Buzzard Point.

Bear Bryant, who served as special agent in charge of the office, was a no-nonsense supervisor with a stellar reputation in the bureau. Agents trusted him because he was a smart boss who sometimes offered sound career advice. Wiser had once gone to Bryant asking for a transfer to a cold-case murder squad. This would have allowed him to hunt down killers. But Bryant, as Wiser later described the conversation, asked him to stay put as a spy hunter for another six months. When the boss "asked" for such things, it was code for *Do this for me*. So Wiser stayed on as a spy catcher.

For that, he was about to be rewarded.

Wiser took a seat in a red leather chair on the other side of Bryant's wooden desk. His boss got right to the point.

"We have a significant penetration of American intelligence, in the CIA," he said. And by "penetration," he meant the worst kind: Someone in the agency was was suspected of selling valuable U.S. secrets to the Russian Federation. "We're not absolutely certain, but we're pretty sure we know who the guy is. It's maybe the most important case the bureau has."

Bryant had every ounce of Wiser's attention.

"Would you be interested in running it?"

Wiser, already a successful spy hunter, was always looking for a bigger challenge—and here it was. Bryant had just offered him the chance to catch a major-league spy, a true villain working for one of America's leading foes. He knew this case, whatever it involved, could make or break his career. Wiser didn't have to think twice before answering.

"Boss," he said, "I've been waiting my whole career for something like this."

Bryant gave him a barebones briefing: Wiser would head a brand-new investigative unit, Major Case Squad 43. His target would be a CIA officer accused of betraying highly classified files to the Russians. The officer, who earned $69,000 a year, had amassed a fortune in unexplained cash. He had traveled the world as a CIA operative—Mexico, Turkey, Italy—and had ties to Colombia, his wife's home country.

Wiser couldn't believe his good luck on that muggy Monday. His boss had just handed him the case of a lifetime. There were veteran counterspies who were vastly more experienced right there in the field office, but Bryant had picked him, and he was thrilled.

The few details he had learned kicked his curious nature into high gear. How could a CIA officer on a government salary put more than $1,000,000 in his bank accounts? Was it espionage? Did he really work for the Russians? The files his target had access to were indeed worth a fortune. But what if it was something else? Could he be a cocaine or emerald smuggler? Wiser knew better than to draw any conclusions at the beginning of an investigation. But as he later said, one thing seemed perfectly clear to him:

"He was guilty of *something*."

Leslie G. Wiser Jr. grew up near Pittsburgh, Pennsylvania, the son of a truck driver and a homemaker with four kids. When Wiser was twelve, he took a trip to Washington, D.C., and found himself on a tour of FBI headquarters. He would later recall walking away with one thought.

"I could *never* do that."

He grew to be six feet tall, ran hurdles on his high school track team, sang in his college choir, and listened to the Beatles. He daydreamed about becoming a lawyer. He didn't know any lawyers, but he had seen one on television he admired: Perry Mason was a fictional defense lawyer in a wildly popular TV drama. Mason took on clients accused of terrible crimes, often murder. His cases always looked hopeless, and his clients seemed destined for prison. But in each episode, Mason's cunning and blistering courtroom cross-examinations helped police identify the real criminal.

In 1979, Wiser, newly married, graduated from the University of Pittsburgh School of Law and joined the U.S. Navy as a lieutenant in the JAG Corps, the legal branch of the Navy. Wiser served on both sides of criminal cases. Sometimes he defended Navy personnel accused of crimes. Other times he prosecuted them. But one case—involving a drunken sailor who fell off a bridge onto railroad tracks—changed his life.

Wiser poured himself into that investigation, thrilled by the hunt for records and the truth. When that case ended, he was hooked on the hunt. Before he left the Navy in 1983, Wiser was offered jobs by the Drug Enforcement Administration, the Naval Investigative Service (now called NCIS), and the FBI.

And so, some seventeen years after a twelve-year-old Les Wiser Jr. declared he could *never* be an FBI agent, he entered duty with the bureau. He began his training at the FBI Academy in Quantico, Virginia.

Ten years later, when Bryant picked him to head the Ames investigation, Wiser was a rising star in the Washington field office. By then, he had two children—a daughter and a son—and an exceedingly patient wife.

"I was gone a lot," Wiser recalled. His wife heard the words "I'll be working late tonight" so often that she just planned on him coming home after dinner. Most mornings he left their home before sunrise, returning twelve hours later. Sometimes he worked through the weekend.

It was all part of the job.

On May 26, 1993, a pair of agents in the Washington field office briefed Wiser on the target of his investigation. They showed him a photo of Rick Ames. Later, he made his way to CIA headquarters for another briefing on Ames. He signed papers that allowed him to look at secret papers in the case. In FBI lingo, this process is called getting "read in."

When he returned to his office, Wiser learned that counterintelligence officials at FBI headquarters were already planning to tail Ames. Wiser believed it was way too early to cover his target's every move. He thought the smarter play was to give Ames some breathing room, watch him from a distance, and see how he operated.

After all, Ames was no ordinary criminal. He was a highly trained professional spy who would be on constant lookout for anyone trying to follow him. Wiser knew that Ames had learned the tricks of the spy trade at the CIA's covert training center, the Farm. There, veteran intelligence officers teach newbies the skills needed by professional spies. Students learn how to pick locks, shoot firearms, build bombs, send and receive secret messages, recruit and handle agents, run roadblocks in cars, spot surveillance teams, and perform other acts of spycraft.

Wiser knew it would be second nature for Ames to be on constant lookout for anyone trying to follow him. So he planned to secretly install a radio beacon in Ames's car, wiretap his phones, mount a video camera in front of his house, and plant hidden cameras and listening devices in his home and office. He ran these plans past Bryant, who backed him all the way.

FBI lawyers obtained permission to spy on Ames from the United States' most secretive court. Judges in the Foreign Intelligence Surveillance Court signed orders that allowed the team to eavesdrop on Ames with electronic spy gear. A high-ranking lawyer in the Department of Justice would also give Wiser's team permission to sneak into Ames's home to look for evidence that he was a spy.

Game on.

CHAPTER 9

Wiser felt a bit like a kid choosing players for a game of capture the flag as he added agents to the NIGHTMOVER team.

From the talented corps of counterintelligence agents in the field office, he selected one to run surveillance operations. He assigned two others to secretly listen in on Ames's phone conversations. Another pair would manage evidence. Wiser assigned one agent to read every page of Sandy Grimes's five-hundred-page timeline so that the NIGHTMOVER group could get a better feel for their target. The team would eventually number more than a dozen agents.

Wiser, who had only recently been promoted to supervisory agent, knew he was working with some of the best spy hunters in the bureau. He decided early on to let those pros do their jobs free of his meddling. As he later put it, they would stay in their lanes, and he would stay in his. His job would be to supervise their work and cheer their progress.

The team took up residence in the Washington Metropolitan Field Office, which overlooked a muddy stretch of the Anacostia River. The building was flanked by violent neighborhoods that in those days helped give Washington, D.C., a dubious nickname: "Murder City." But for agents, the decaying FBI building had its own horrors. Rats were plentiful. One agent discovered a family of roaches living in a stapler. Wiser once found a dead mouse in the take-out bin of a vending machine.

Squad 43 moved into a carpeted space across the hallway from Bryant's corner office on the eleventh floor. This dumpy rectangle, with a wall of old sound-proofing material, would serve as NIGHTMOVER head-quarters for more than 250 days. In the months to come, other agents in the office would be dying to know what they were up to in there. FBI counterspies knew better than to ask what another squad was working on, but some did anyway.

"When they asked," Wiser said, "we said we were

working on the *X-Files*." (The fictional TV drama featured two FBI agents seeking answers to mysteries involving UFOs and other paranormal activities.) The team's response to such questions was clearly a joke, but they were sending a serious message to others in the office: "We can't talk about it."

The NIGHTMOVER investigation began slowly, as Wiser intended. He wanted to get a feel for Ames, to see if he was a good spy. He knew his investigation was over if Ames ever realized the FBI was watching him. Wiser knew Ames could destroy evidence and flee the country overnight. He also knew that the SVR often set up emergency plans to sneak assets away to safety.

On June 3, 1993, Wiser sent in the Gs.

The members of the Special Surveillance Group were talented FBI employees—none of them agents—who looked like ordinary people. They were investigative specialists who could pose as trash collectors, pizza deliverers, a TV repair crew, a couple of young lovers kissing in a park, runners putting in some roadwork, even an old woman struggling down a sidewalk with a cane. The Gs—about fifty strong—were legendary for their camera work. They could shoot photos and videos from long distances, in any weather. And they could do it while tailing their subjects in cars. As Bear Bryant once noted of them, "They can follow a fly through an ice storm."

Wiser gave the order for the Gs to keep their eyes on Ames. His superiors didn't give him a "blank check" for round-the-clock surveillance. But he put them on the road two shifts a day. Wiser wanted the Gs to follow their target by car to see where he might be going before and after work. But this surveillance was nothing like what you see on TV. On television, police tail their subject in one car and the crooks never seem to notice them. The Gs were pros. They folded into traffic with several cars, keeping track of their target from in front and behind.

The CIA teaches spies like Ames all the moves to detect surveillance. These moves are called SDRs—surveillance detection runs. For instance, if trained spies think someone is following them in a car, they might take a mental note of the auto's brand, color, and style—then make an abrupt turn into a gas station, cross a few lanes, and zoom down an exit ramp, circling back the other way. Then they would scan traffic for the car they had seen before. No matter where they go, spies know to look out for any driver's face and vehicle that seem to turn up near them more than once.

The Gs reported to Wiser that Ames had done nothing suspicious.

Wiser sent an FBI technical agent dressed as a phone company employee to Ames's neighborhood. The undercover agent pretended to be working on a telephone line. But his real mission was to secretly mount a video camera on the phone pole and point its lens at the front of the Ames home. In FBI lingo, this pole camera served as the "eye" of the NIGHTMOVER team. Now they could record every movement Ames made as he came and went from his house.

The team also rented a vacant house about a block from Ames's place. This rental served as a command post for NIGHTMOVER's eavesdropping. A videocassette recorder in the house captured footage from the pole camera.

Wiser, a devout Presbyterian, sometimes prayed for guidance in the privacy of his home. His target was smart, sophisticated, and wary. So far, Ames had made no mistake that might reveal him as a Russian spy. The stakes of this game were terribly high because Ames still worked for the CIA. Every day offered him a new chance to steal secrets from the deep vaults of the United States and sell them to the Russians.

But the NIGHTMOVER team enjoyed one big advantage: They were the hunters, and Ames seemed clueless that he was the hunted.

CHAPTER 10

Rick Ames's first act in the CIA had turned him into an expert on all things KGB. His second act was to perform that job while looting the agency of its secrets and selling them to the KGB. His final act at the CIA came after the 1991 collapse of the Soviet Union, when his superiors reassigned him to a new job in the agency.

Ames went to work in the Counternarcotics Center, known as the CNC, where he and other CIA officers labored to break up the global trade in heroin and other illegal drugs. The move took Ames away from all counter-intelligence matters. While he had not been given access to files on the CIA's Soviet assets since 1986, and would rarely rub elbows with those who did, his new job gave Ames approved access to Russian intelligence officers.

They too worked in counternarcotics. And they would team up with the CIA in their mutual war against dangerous drugs.

Wiser and the NIGHTMOVER team hoped to find evidence of Ames's espionage in his office. So in the wee hours of Friday, June 25, 1993, Wiser and other agents drove over to the CIA. A half-moon shined over the CIA compound as they approached the agency's New Headquarters Building, its arched glass roof glowing an eerie green.

Dan Payne, a key member of the CIA's internal mole hunt, met them at the door. The agents, posing as CIA officers in blue employee badges, passed the security checkpoint, turned down a corridor, and caught an elevator to the basement. There, Payne guided them to room GV06, home of the Counternarcotics Center.

The CNC was a big, open room full of desks. The agents walked across that space to one of two private offices. A sign on the door read RICK AMES. Its interior was painted beige, with gray trim. The ceiling was made of white acoustic tiles with tiny holes in them to absorb sound.

The undercover FBI agents stared at Ames's desk, which looked like a disaster area. It was littered with empty coffee cups, books, reports, notebooks, and 144 secret documents (totaling hundreds of pages) that had nothing to do with Ames's new job.

One of the agents used a Polaroid camera to shoot instant photos of the desk. Then, working like archaeologists, the agents very carefully lifted each stack of papers to make copies. When they were finished, they studied their photos and placed the papers precisely as they had found them. FBI technical agents, skilled at electronic surveillance, bugged Ames's phone and mounted a tiny video camera in a ceiling tile above his desk.

Back at the field office, Wiser studied the documents his team had copied. Ten of them were classified top secret. One was a CIA report that detailed ways in which the nuclear submarines of the Soviet Union, later the Russian Federation, had avoided detection by the U.S. Navy. It was plain to Wiser that Ames planned to sell these national defense secrets to the SVR, a clear act of criminal espionage.

Wiser's next goal was to tail Ames without him realizing it.

The best way to do that, he knew, was to hide a radio beacon in Ames's Jaguar. Wiser thought about sending a team of technical agents over to the sprawling parking lot at CIA headquarters, but that was too dangerous. If Ames caught them, or heard from a co-worker that someone had been looking under the hood of his Jag, it would tip him off that he was under investigation.

Paul Redmond, who had supervised the Ames mole-hunt team for the CIA, offered Wiser some advice. He encouraged him to think of Ames as a spy working for the KGB. To catch a spy, he said, you have to think like a spy. Wiser took the advice to heart. And he came up with an idea right out of a James Bond movie.

His plan was to separate Ames from his car for long enough to plant the beacon under his hood. But where? Wiser thought the J. Edgar Hoover Building, headquarters of the FBI, would be just perfect. But first he had to get some help from Ames's boss in the CNC, Dave Edger, who had secretly been briefed on the Ames investigation.

On July 20, 1993, Edger asked Rick to drive them to a meeting they were to attend at FBI headquarters. A couple of FBI agents had invited them over to discuss the Black Sea Initiative. This was a plan to wipe out the opium trade between Eastern Europe and the Middle East. Edger told Ames that his car was in the shop, so they would have to take his Jaguar over to the Hoover Building.

At the FBI, Ames parked his Jag next to a cobblestone courtyard. He and Edger caught an elevator upstairs for their meeting, which was supposed to last several hours. Once they were upstairs, an FBI agent casually walked out to Ames's car, slipped behind the wheel, and inserted a duplicate key into the ignition. (He had gotten the key from the makers of Ames's Jaguar.) The agent drove the Jag into the FBI's underground garage. There, a team of tech agents lifted the hood and hid the transmitter inside.

Now that the Gs could keep a closer eye on Ames in his Jaguar, Wiser wanted to get a good look at his suspect's garbage.

When you think about it, the stuff you throw into the trash says a lot about you. Sure, there are eggshells and coffee grounds and smelly cat litter. But people also throw out receipts, old bank statements, and other papers they might not want people to see. Who figures that someone would ever go through their trash? But it's a trick right out of the FBI playbook.

It's called a "trash cover."

Wiser liked the idea of pulling Ames's trash to see if it might provide some clues. But when he ran the idea past Bryant, his boss declared it way too risky. Bryant pointed out that if Ames was a night owl, he might look out his bedroom window in the middle of the night and see the FBI grabbing his garbage can. Wiser saw Bryant's point, so for the next few weeks, the Gs kept a close watch on Ames's home at night and discovered that Ames did smoke late at night. But Wiser still wanted to make off with his trash.

The NIGHTMOVER team obtained a trash can identical to Ames's, which they would use as a decoy. The Gs, under Wiser's watch, practiced jumping out of a van, quietly grabbing one can, and leaving the decoy in its place. They could make the switch in seconds. When Wiser brought this up with Bryant, his boss was still uneasy about using the tactic. But he agreed that Wiser could give it a try.

Wiser's team performed flawless trash covers three times in August 1993. Each time they carried Ames's trash bin to a nearby building, spilled out the contents, and picked through it looking for clues. Each time they pulled carefully timed switcheroos, taking back their decoy can and replacing it with Ames's can. But they found nothing of any value, it was all just trash.

Bryant ordered Wiser to stop the risky trash covers.

That summer, the NIGHTMOVER team came up with

a new and less messy plan. They would work with the CIA to find a highly classified document of great interest to the Russians. They would make sure that someone in the agency delivered the file to Ames's office. The FBI could then record Ames's reaction with the video camera mounted above his desk. If Ames read the file and smuggled it out of the CIA compound, they might be able to arrest him for espionage.

When agents later watched the videotape, they saw the document being delivered to Ames, who leafed through the file. They also saw Ames toss the document into a box for outgoing files and lean back in his chair. Then he took a nap.

Wiser and his team had once again come up empty-handed.

Then there was that terrible day—September 9, 1993—the day Ames repeatedly slipped past Wiser's surveilling agents. The day the Gs lost him twice on the highway. The day Ames zoomed out of the CIA compound and lost them. The day the FBI pilot failed to get his plane into the air in time to follow Ames. And the day that Wiser got chewed out for all of those missed cues.

Yes, that day. The worst day of Wiser's FBI career.

CHAPTER **11**

The directors of the FBI and CIA were furious with the NIGHTMOVER team's performance on the 9th of September, 1993.

Now came more trouble. Wiser's boss, Bear Bryant, was taking heat for the NIGHTMOVER team's surveillance activities. Parishioners at a church near Ames's home were complaining about strange men—the Gs—hanging out in their parking lot. Another neighbor was asking local police about a mysterious plane that kept circling the neighborhood. It was one of the FBI's "Nightstalker" aircraft.

Wiser worried that Ames might get word of such peculiarities and realize he was under investigation. He felt enormous pressure from senior FBI executives. One more foul-up, he knew, might prompt them to yank him off the case.

"How long are these guys going to stand behind me," Wiser wondered, "before they decide they need a new quarterback?"

He tried to put such thoughts out of his mind. But Wiser was a new supervisor with few longtime FBI buddies to count on for moral support. "I didn't have a lot of lifelines," he later explained. But when he walked into the field office on the morning of September 10, a sticky Friday in the nation's capital, he got a pleasant surprise. The NIGHTMOVER team stood behind him. Special Agent Mike Anderson, a seasoned counterintelligence veteran with deep knowledge of the KGB and SVR, helped Wiser examine the previous day's mistakes and gave him encouragement.

"He told me that the plan was good, but the execution was not," Wiser recalled. "We agreed we could fix the flawed execution. He was selfless, calm, and reasonable; he was just what I needed that morning."

The foul-ups that dogged the NIGHTMOVER team came with one upside. Wiser now got the green light to put surveillance teams on Ames 24/7. Before that, he explained, his budget-conscious bosses had only let him put tails on his target twice a day.

Wiser decided to quit playing it safe and follow his instincts. It was time to go big or go home.

"I didn't feel I had much to lose at that point," he said.

Wiser decided to send the Gs over to Ames's home one more time to do a trash cover. He knew that Bryant had ordered him to abandon the risky tactic earlier that summer. But Wiser, hoping for better luck, ignored his boss's direct order.

This is rarely a smart move by any agent.

When Anderson heard about Wiser's plan, he approached Wiser.

"Didn't the boss tell you not to do that?"

"Mike," Wiser replied, "this is on me. Just keep your mouth shut."

The NIGHTMOVER team, secretly listening to all of Ames's phone conversations, knew he was heading to Ankara, Turkey, on September 13, 1993, for a conference on the global drug trade. This offered a good chance to pull their target's trash without being caught.

For his part, Ames was enjoying his new work. He had organized the conference in Turkey himself, inviting intelligence officers from the United States and other nations, including Russia, to discuss the Black Sea counter-narcotics program.

On the final night of the Black Sea conference, Ames got drunk and gave a speech. He preached to his fellow spies about a new era of brotherly cooperation. Later, Ames was so pleased with the success of his conference that he danced with a CIA secretary.

"I felt a tremendous sense of accomplishment," Ames would later recall to the author Pete Earley. "For a few sweet moments, I felt good abbut the agency and myself."

As Ames partied in Turkey, the NIGHTMOVER team prepared to make its move.

Shortly after midnight, Wiser walked into the FBI's covert warehouse in Fairfax, Virginia—home to the Gs' trash-cover team. They were now experts at jumping in and out of their van. One agent would grab a trash can and carry it back to the van as the other planted the decoy and jumped back in. Wiser was pleased to see they could perform the feat in as little as eleven seconds.

Wiser wished them good luck. He knew that with Ames out of the country, the only people home at his residence were Rosario and Paul. He also knew that if either of them saw strange men stealing their trash bin, his investigation—indeed, his life as a spycatcher—would probably come to a bruising end.

At about 2:30 A.M., four hours before sunup, a black van crept into Ames's leafy neighborhood in Arlington. Agents had disabled the lights inside the van. Now its headlights blinked off. The driver eased the van to the curb at 2512 North Randolph Street and stopped. Two men wearing sweatshirts, jeans, and sneakers leaped out and expertly performed the trash cover. Then the van pulled quietly into the night, reaching the FBI warehouse about twenty minutes later.

Special Agent Dell Spry was waiting for them. The team had built a V-shaped plywood chute that was held up by sawhorses. FBI employees dressed in hazmat suits pushed handfuls of Ames's trash down the chute and picked through the rubbish with gloved hands.

Spry watched as one of the Gs pulled out a yellow scrap of paper. It was part of a Post-it Note. They could make out two handwritten words: "meet at." Soon they found other scraps, with more words. They pieced them together, finding two notes in Ames's handwriting. Spry, a highly trained counterspy, could plainly see that these were drafts of a note.

"That *thar*," Spry declared with a strong Southern drawl, "is a *spy* note!"

Spry figured the final version of the note went into a dead drop for the Russians. The key portion of the drafts read: "I am ready to meet at B on 1 Oct."

The note, as deciphered by agents, was a clear signal that Ames planned to travel on the first day of October to Bogotá, Colombia, to meet his Russian handler. Agents knew that Ames was familiar with the capital city in his wife's homeland.

Spry rang Wiser at about 3:30 A.M. Wiser picked up, groggy, hoping for good news. The two men couldn't talk about their case over an unsecure phone line. But Spry, in his unmistakable drawl, discreetly let him know he had something of great interest at the office.

"Do I have time to shower?" Wiser asked.

"Yeah," Spry said.

Wiser crept out of bed, shaved, showered, and made his way to the office from his home in Bowie, Maryland, before sunrise. There, he enjoyed a long look at a photo enlargement of the note all pieced together.

This was a big moment for NIGHTMOVER, especially after all the things that had gone wrong. The Post-it Note scraps, Wiser recalled years later, were a huge find. "Because until that point," he said, "we really didn't have anything solid that said this guy was a spy." Now, he said, "we knew we had a spy—and that he was active."

Each piece of evidence in a criminal case is like a brick. Gather enough bricks, and you can build a wall of evidence to

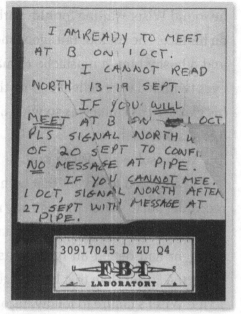

I AM READY TO MEET AT B ON 1 OCT.
    I CANNOT READ NORTH 13-19 SEPT.
    IF YOU WILL MEET AT B ON 1 OCT. PLS SIGNAL NORTH W OF 20 SEPT TO CONFI. NO MESSAGE AT PIPE.
    IF YOU CANNOT MEE. 1 OCT, SIGNAL NORTH AFTER 27 SEPT WITH MESSAGE AT PIPE.

30917045 D ZU Q4
FBI LABORATORY

FBI agents made a startling discovery when they picked through the Ames family trash: Rick Ames had thrown away a draft note that set up a secret meeting with his Russian spy friends in Bogotá, Colombia.

show to a criminal court jury. But some bricks are bigger than others and carry more weight. The NIGHTMOVER team knew it had collected one good brick to begin building that wall. Still, Wiser's great hope was to obtain a photograph of Ames loading a dead drop with secret files. Now *that*, he knew, would be a very big brick.

When Bryant reached his office later that morning,

he found Wiser waiting for him with a goofy expression on his face. The six-foot-tall agent had a head of dark hair and a bushy brown mustache to match. His bright blue eyes twinkled with delight behind the big dark frames of his glasses. His smile was so wide and toothy he looked like a jack-o'-lantern.

"We've solved it," Wiser said.

He admitted to Bryant that he had disobeyed his direct order not to search through any more of Ames's trash.

Bryant, who would ordinarily have been furious that an agent had defied an order, was so pleased to hear about the Post-it Note that he let it go. He would later describe Wiser's failure to follow his order as "a marvelous piece of insubordination."

Later that day, key figures on the CIA mole-hunt team—Paul Redmond, Sandy Grimes, and Jeanne Vertefeuille—drove to the FBI's Washington field office to take a look at the Post-it Note. Spry would later recall that day as one of the finest in his long career in the FBI. He said Redmond spotted him from across the room and launched himself in Spry's direction.

"Walked right up to me," he said. "Hugged me, kissed me on the cheek."

CHAPTER 12

Members of the NIGHTMOVER team listened
in as Rick Ames placed a call on September 19, 1993. Their
target made reservations to fly to Bogotá ten days later,
with a return to Virginia in early October.

Wiser assembled a team of roughly fifteen people,
including himself, a handful of other FBI agents, and
six CIA officers. They made the 2,400-mile flight to Bogotá ahead of Ames to prepare their surveillance. They
dressed to blend in as tourists in the tropical town. The
team didn't know where Ames would meet his handler,
so they staked out several spots, including shops and
cafes, near the Russian embassy.

The team's goal was to capture images of Ames
meeting with his SVR contact—possibly even accepting

money. That evidence alone would mean game over for Rick Ames.

On September 29, 1993, the day Ames was to leave for Bogotá, agents listening to the wiretaps heard him call Rosario from his car phone.

"There's news," he said.

"Oh . . ."

"Yeah," he said, "not going."

It was clear to the FBI that Ames had driven past one of the signal sites that the SVR had set up in Washington. This one, which agents would later confirm was called "Smile," was a mailbox between the Embassy of the Russian Federation and its compound at Mount Alto, where its diplomats and spies lived. Ames had then driven to a dead drop to retrieve instructions, which let him know the SVR had canceled their meeting in Bogotá.

Wiser returned to Washington with the rest of the team a few days later. He discovered that in his absence, Bryant had ordered the Gs to quit following Ames by car. It was now much too risky. Tailing Ames all the way to a dead drop and shooting photos of him would have been a major success, but following him around in the D.C. area could ruin the investigation. Wiser knew that highly skilled SVR officers also kept tabs on Ames's movements. If they saw the Gs following Ames to a dead drop or signal site, they would probably shut down the Ames operation, put him on a plane, and fly him to a hero's welcome in Russia.

That was a nightmare Wiser couldn't risk. His team continued to listen closely to Ames's phone conversations. He hoped the wiretaps would help his team plan its next moves.

On October 3, 1993, unbeknownst to the FBI, Ames made his way to a dead drop in Wheaton Regional Park in the Maryland suburbs north of Washington. He retrieved a handwritten message from the SVR on a scrap of the *Washington Times* newspaper. The message gave Ames a new rendezvous date of November 1, 1993, in Bogotá. Inside the package was another brick of cash.

The SVR instructed Ames to confirm he would make the meeting in Colombia. To do so, he was to leave a chalk slash on the mailbox at Thirty-seventh and R Streets—the signal site named Smile.

Later that day, Ames phoned Rosario from the car. "All is well," he said.

"Financially, too?"

"Ah, yeah," he said. "Wait 'til I get there."

The FBI, listening carefully to Ames's call home, thought Rosario seemed to know quite a lot about her husband's financial dealings with the Russians.

Three days later, in the early hours of October 6, the Gs once again quietly made off with Ames's trash can. This time, they recovered a typewriter-ribbon cartridge. Wiser would later roll the ribbon out of the cartridge onto spools. The letters appeared backward, so agents pulled a mirror off a wall in a nearby office and held it beneath the ribbon. This allowed Wiser to read and dictate each word to a secretary, who took notes in shorthand.

"In the movie," Wiser joked to his fellow agents, "[we are] going to send this [ribbon] over to the lab and they're going to have this big computer and it will spit it out and give us the answer. It's actually pretty funny that we're sitting here doing this."

The ribbon revealed two notes that Ames had tapped out to the SVR.

His first note confirmed a meeting the previous year with the SVR in Caracas, Venezuela. That message, riddled with typos, looked as if Ames had been drunk when he wrote it. He had closed that message, "Until we meet in Caracas . . . K." Agents guessed that the K stood for Ames's code name.

Indeed, it did. Ames had come up with the name himself: Kolokol. It was the Russian word for "bell."

Ames's second note shared a few words about his beloved wife.

Rosario, he wrote, supported his work for the SVR.

CHAPTER 13

The NIGHTMOVER team had been waiting for months to take a secret look inside Ames's home. Finally, it got permission. Deputy U.S. Attorney General Philip B. Heymann signed a secret order that allowed agents to sneak into Ames's roomy house to search for evidence.

Wiser wanted no surprises when they got inside, so the agents prepared for the "sneak and peek" operation with many days of research. They found a copy of the home's floor plan in a real-estate brochure. They also located another house with the same layout. In a stroke of luck, its owner was a retired FBI agent, and he was happy to let agents study the interior of his home.

Days before entering Ames's house, an FBI technical agent sneaked onto the property and inserted a mechanism into the keyhole of the cellar door's lock. The device allowed agents to make a key for their covert entry.

Agents waited until Columbus Day weekend in 1993 to make their move. They picked that date because they knew the Ames family would be out of town. Rick, Rosario, and their son had flown to Pensacola, Florida, nearly a thousand miles away, to attend the wedding of Rick's nephew. Young Paul was to serve as ring bearer.

The NIGHTMOVER team had secretly enlisted the help of one of Ames's neighbors, who cooperated with agents and promised not to tell anyone about their assistance. That neighbor allowed the team to gather at the house in advance of the sneak and peek.

At 1 A.M., under a crescent moon, a team of agents crept onto Ames's property. The primary search team—a technical agent named Tom Murray and agents Mike Mitchell and Rudy Guerin—hoped to search the house and shoot photos of any evidence they might find. A secondary team of technical agents would plant listening devices throughout the dwelling—even in Rick and Rosario's bedroom.

The agents, armed with their key, made their way to the cellar door. But to their dismay, they discovered that someone had broken off a key in the lock, barring their entry. So they launched what is called a "black bag job." A highly skilled agent equipped with lock-picking tools went to work on the back door. Forty-five minutes after the team's arrival on Ames's property, the FBI slipped inside the house and eased the door shut.

Only a handful of agents took part in the search and bugging operation. Over the years, the FBI had learned that the more people that are sent into a target's home, the more chances of error there are. Agents could accidentally break things or leave footprints—and sometimes even their own gear—behind. There's an old story in the FBI about a sneak-and-peek team that corralled a cat that they believed had escaped from the house they were searching and left it inside. Later they learned their target didn't own a cat.

The NIGHTMOVER team moved inch by inch through the dark living room. Agents covered the street-facing windows with blackout cloths. This way, if a neighbor looked out their window in the middle of the night, they wouldn't see flashlights cutting through the interior of the Ames home. The last thing Wiser wanted was a suspicious neighbor phoning 911 to report a burglary in progress. But the NIGHTMOVER team was ready, should that happen. One of the agents had a contact in the Arlington Police Department who could stop his officers from walking into the search.

Tom Murray, a computer expert, made his way to Ames's study and found his target's computer. He copied the hard drive and data from several diskettes, portable storage devices that were in use at that time.

Rudy Guerin had studied the floor plan of the house so carefully that he felt like he lived there. Yet he kept bumping into furniture. He moved through the house, penlight in hand, to Rick Ames's bedroom.

Guerin found a chest of drawers and eased the top drawer open. He observed a tangle of stale socks and used handkerchiefs. He dug around until he found a crumpled note scribbled on a piece of the *Washington Times*. Guerin didn't know it at the time, but this was the message left for Ames at his dead drop in Wheaton Regional Park. The note began, "Are ready to meet at a city well known to you on 1 Nov."

Guerin carried the note into the bathroom, where Agent Mitchell had set up a document camera built into a suitcase. When the case was opened, it erected a frame with an auto-focus lens. The agents closed the bathroom door, slid the note under the camera, and snapped a photo. The bright flash blanched the bathroom like lightning.

Now Guerin crept back to Ames's bedroom, carefully tucking the SVR note back where he had found it. He then made his way to Ames's closet, where he nearly gagged. Ames's clothes, saturated by years of cigarette smoke, smelled terrible. Guerin slipped his hands into the pockets of Ames's suits, finding a 1991 note with the name and phone number of a KGB officer in Vienna, Austria.

The NIGHTMOVER team finished its search, locked the house behind them, and pulled away at 4:30 A.M. Once underway, an agent radioed a single word to Wiser back at the field office: "Okay."

This let him know they were clear.

CHAPTER 14

On Sunday morning, just a few hours after the NIGHTMOVER team completed its search of the Ames home, Les Wiser took a call. Tom Murray was on the line from the field office. He had news.

"I've got some stuff I think you'll be interested in," he said.

Wiser made his way down for a look. He found Murray in the squad room, a sterile, carpeted space full of metal desks. There, Murray showed him the trove of evidence he had found on Ames's computer and storage devices, including the names of CIA employees, assets, and operations. It was clear to Wiser that Ames had sold these closely guarded secrets to the SVR.

Murray also found a letter that Ames had written

to the SVR the previous year. It showed what a slave to money he had become. Ames complained to his Russian pals in a way that only a spoiled-rich criminal could. He whined about running low on the bricks of cash they had been paying him. He described this as "a very tight and unpleasant situation" that had forced him to sell stocks and a certificate of deposit from a Swiss bank.

"Therefore," Ames wrote, "I will need as much cash delivered in [the] Pipe [dead drop] as you think can be accommodated"; he misspelled the last word. Ames noted that the hiding space at the dead drop was probably big enough to hold $100,000.

Wiser found it sobering that Ames's secrets were fetching so much cash. He knew it would take two years for an honest CIA officer to bring home that much pay.

On Tuesday, October 12, 1993, a couple of days after agents searched Ames's home, they listened to a conversation captured by a bug in Ames's kitchen.

"I have to take off early to put a signal down," Ames told his wife.

"You have to what?" Rosario said.

"They would like confirmation that I am coming."

"Who?"

Agents couldn't make out Ames's answer. But it was clear to them he was talking about the SVR.

"Do you have to lay something down in the afternoon?" Rosario asked.

"No, uh-uh," Ames told her. "Just mark the signal."

"Why didn't you do it today, for God's sake?" she asked.

"I should have, except it was raining like crazy." He explained that the deadline to mark the signal was the fourteenth.

"Tomorrow's the thirteenth," she said, sounding annoyed.

"Uh-huh."

"Well, honey," she said, "I hope you didn't screw up."

This casual chat staggered the writer David Wise, who wrote one of the first books on the Ames case. "Rick and Rosario," he wrote, "were discussing espionage in the same cadences that husbands and wives might use in talking about who would nip into 7-Eleven to pick up a quart of milk."

Les Wiser took a more practical view of that husband-and-wife chat. It was clear to him that Rosario was aware of Ricks' espionage—but she was merely a bit player in this drama. Wiser knew that Ames would do almost anything to protect his wife and son. So he began to form a plan, in the event that they arrested Ames.

He would use Rosario's freedom as a bargaining chip.

"We wanted to catch that sicko," he said of Ames. "Normal people don't go out and drive someplace and put a chalk mark on a mailbox." And normal wives, he said, don't chew their husbands out for not pushing themselves out in a pouring rain to put a signal down for a bunch of Russian spies.

On October 13 at 6:22 A.M, Ames eased his Jag out onto North Randolph Street. He returned twenty-two minutes later, according to video collected by the pole camera.

It seemed clear to the NIGHTMOVER team that Ames had driven to the Smile signal site. The Gs confirmed it shortly after Ames returned to his home. They drove past the mailbox and observed a fresh chalk mark.

One more brick for that wall of evidence.

The mark Ames put down let the SVR know he would meet them in Bogotá on November 1, 1993.

The mark also sent Wiser into action. He made plane reservations for Bogotá. For the second time, he would lead a team of agents to Colombia's capital city. This time, Wiser hoped, the NIGHTMOVER team could follow Ames to a meeting with his SVR handler.

The FBI, then at war with Colombia's deadly Medellín cocaine cartel, did not tell the Colombian government that a team of agents was heading its way. They would fly to Bogotá in their true names, but would pose as tourists. They would take no badges or guns.

But they'd pack plenty of cameras.

This mailbox served as the "Smile" signal sight. Ames and Russian spies drew chalk lines on the box to indicate they had stashed new messages in dead drops all over Washington, D.C.

Ames took off for Bogotá on October 30, 1993.

In the days before he left, the FBI secretly listened to a series of chats between Rick and Rosario Ames. She did not sound worried about his safety. But she seemed quite concerned about the cash he planned to smuggle back into the United States. She urged him to put the money in a carry-on bag, not in his checked luggage.

"You're going to have to be a little more imaginative," she told him the day before he left. "You always have this envelope with this big hunk [of cash], I mean really." The next day, she said, "I don't want you to bring back anything that will make them want to look in your luggage."

Agents, especially the men, chuckled as they listened to Rosario browbeat her husband.

The day before Ames's trip, he told Rosario what to say if someone from the CIA phoned the house: "If anybody happens to call, you tell them I went up to Annapolis [Maryland]. You don't have to explain why."

Ames gave her that cover story because he didn't want the CIA to know he was in Colombia. He had not told his bosses he was leaving the country, a serious breach of CIA regulations.

Agent Rudy Guerin flew down to Florida to make sure Ames caught his connecting flight from Miami to Bogotá.

The FBI worried that someone from the SVR might walk into Miami International Airport, stroll past Ames with a wink, and casually pick up Ames's suitcase full of

CIA files. The Russian spy would go one way and Ames would fly down to Bogotá. There, the SVR would wine and dine him before sending him packing with another big brick of hundred-dollar bills.

Guerin did tail Ames to an airport bar, but there was no clandestine meeting. No exchange of suitcases. Ames took a seat, knocked back a few rounds of booze, and puffed on his cancer sticks. Then he wobbled off to board his plane to Bogotá.

Guerin phoned Squad 43 to report that Ames was on his way. He also let them know their target was carrying a laptop.

CHAPTER 15

A rainstorm rolled over the Andes Mountains and splashed the streets of Bogotá in the early evening of November 1, 1993. Rick Ames, caught in the rain shower, walked into the Unicentro mall in his drenched trench coat. The sprawling shopping center, with its stores and cinemas, stood 8,400 feet above sea level.

At 6:45 P.M., Ames strode through the mall looking like a very wet spy.

Special Agent Yolanda M. Larson, a Spanish-speaking member of the NIGHTMOVER team, sat at a table near the mall's bowling alley, called Bolicentro. Built into her briefcase was a video camera that captured images of Ames walking past in an overcoat, his hair slicked by the rain. Larson thought her target seemed to be looking for someone.

Indeed he was.

Ames had arrived fifteen minutes early for his 7 P.M. meeting with his SVR handler, whom he knew as "Andre." The man's real name was Yuri Karetkin. The SVR had designated Bolicentro its primary meeting place, known by Russian spies as an "iron site." But by 7:30 P.M. their favorite American spy, convinced Andre was a no-show, made his way out of the mall.

Larson captured images of Ames with her briefcase camera, but she failed to get the money shot: Ames meeting his handler. However, she had been there earlier, a little before 6 P.M., when a curious-looking fellow who seemed to be searching for someone walked past. Larson captured excellent images of this man, whom the NIGHTMOVER team would later identify as Karetkin.

She reported the Ames sighting to Wiser, who had set up a command post in a nearby hotel room. Wiser and the other agents couldn't understand how Ames and his handler had missed each other.

Ames phoned home later that night from Bogotá. He placed the call from his mother-in-law's place. Cecilia

Teams of FBI agents searched for Ames in Bogotá, Colombia, on two different occasions in the fall of 1993. An FBI agent captured this image at the Unicentro mall using a video camera built into a briefcase.

Dupuy de Casas was there with him when he placed the call.

"I had a short meeting this evening," he said.

A lie.

"Did you really meet?" Rosario asked.

"Uh-huh."

Rosario grew angry with Ames, thinking he had missed the meeting. Indeed, her instincts were spot-on. He had missed his meeting. He was supposed to meet

Karetkin at 6 P.M., not 7 P.M. So Ames and Andre had been there at different times.

Later in the conversation, Rosario asked her husband what he was doing the next day.

"I'm gonna do a little shopping in Unicentro," he said, "then I have meetings in the afternoon, and then out in the evening as well."

"Okay," she said, "just be careful. And you swear to me that nothing went wrong?"

"Yeah. That's right."

"You swear?"

"Uh-huh."

"Well, you don't sound too sure," Rosario said. "You're sure? Sure, right?

"Sure."

"You wouldn't lie to me, would you?"

"No. No. Okay?"

"Okay."

"Okay, good," Ames said.

Spies like Ames, who lie for a living, pride themselves on being able to tell a whopper and make it stick.

"Just rest assured," he said. "Okay?"

"Okay," she said. "Be careful tomorrow."

Later that day, Wiser took a call from Mike Anderson, back at the Washington field office.

"Hey, they made the meet," he told Wiser.

"They did?"

"Yeah, they made the meet."

Anderson did not elaborate over the long-distance phone line. The lines could not be trusted. This left Wiser to rack his brain. *How did we miss that meeting? We were at the right place, and Ames was there? Now what do we do?*

By lying to his wife, mostly to avoid getting an earful, Ames had accidentally thrown off the FBI team listening to his calls.

The following day, Wiser sent agents all over Bogotá to look for Ames. But they never found him. So they did not see him meet Karetkin at the Unicentro mall. They did not see the two men make their way to the Russian Embassy. And they most certainly did not see Ames and Karetkin make their way to a private room, where Karetkin paid Ames $50,000 in U.S. cash.

On the third of November, a Wednesday, Wiser and Special Agent Mike Donner drove out to the airport. They had developed a contact there who gave the two agents behind-the-scenes access to Ames's luggage.

"We got in and got the luggage out of the baggage [area], and we looked at it," Wiser recalled. They had hoped to find cash hidden inside Ames's bags. They had brought a camera to take a literal money shot. They had also hoped to photograph the serial numbers on individual bills. This might help them trace the cash back to the Russian Federation. But there was no money in Ames's luggage.

He flew home carrying the fifty grand in his carry-on bag, just as Rosario had told him to.

On November 3, the FBI listened in on a conversation in which Ames told his wife they were about to get a major infusion of cash. The SVR had promised him four payments in 1994 that would feather their nest quite nicely. Then there was this: "They're holding one million, nine hundred thousand dollars for me in Moscow."

The writer David Wise tallied all the payments made or promised to Ames by the KGB and SVR during his nine years of work for Moscow. It came to $4.6 million.

CHAPTER 16

In the late fall of 1993, Les Wiser heard troubling news: Ames had found a weakness in the CIA's computer system.

Computers in Ames's department, the agency's Counternarcotics Center, were equipped with storage ports. This meant that Ames could now download classified files onto diskettes and carry them out of the CIA.

One night soon after, the NIGHTMOVER team made its way to the CIA to take a peek at Ames's desk. Sure enough, they found diskettes at his workstation. Agents checked the diskettes and found files containing hundreds of multipage documents. Ames had left evidence of his betrayal just sitting out in the open on his desk.

They copied the diskettes and later printed the files at the Washington field office. The stack of papers towered more than two feet high, at roughly six thousand pages. Wiser and the rest of the NIGHTMOVER team knew that Ames planned to hand over the diskettes to the Russians.

"[That was] kind of a game changer," he recalled. The agents pursuing Ames all knew they could never, ever let him pass those highly restricted papers to the SVR.

Soon after, Wiser got more bad news. The Gs had spotted cars with Russian diplomatic license plates—clearly SVR officers—driving into the zones where the surveillance teams roamed. Wiser worried that the SVR was onto the FBI and might try to sneak Ames out of the country. Senior officials in the FBI feared a repeat of one of the bureau's most embarrassing moments—the Edward Lee Howard fiasco.

Howard was a former CIA officer who fell under suspicion of being a Soviet spy in 1985. The FBI put Howard, who lived in New Mexico, under what is called "bumper lock" surveillance. They let Howard know they were watching him, and they tailed him everywhere he went. They were hoping to build a criminal case against him.

One night that September, Howard and his wife went to dinner. His wife drove on the way home, with

Howard sitting in the front passenger seat. When she rounded a bend on a dark road, Howard pitched himself out the door and rolled out of sight. His wife then activated a dummy to take the front seat in Howard's place, a trick called a "Jack in the Box." The agents following the couple saw nothing, partly because Howard had disabled the car's interior lights. The former agent defected to Moscow with the help of the KGB.

Wiser worried that the Russians might have figured out that Ames was under investigation. If the SVR was able to sneak Ames out of the country, there might not be enough soap and water in the world to wash the egg off Wiser's face.

At Christmastime 1993, Wiser got more troubling news: Ames was planning an official CIA trip to Moscow as part of his counter-narcotics work. Wiser gulped at the very thought of it. The U.S. government would become a laughingstock if Ames made his way to Russia and defected, becoming a Russian citizen. Wiser could only imagine how crushing it would feel to see Ames in a press conference in Moscow, news cameras rolling, bragging to the world that he had outsmarted the FBI and CIA for nine years.

Wiser spoke to CIA mole-hunt supervisor Paul

Redmond about Ames's planned trip to Moscow. Both agreed there was no way they were letting Ames go to Russia. They secretly postponed Ames's trip a few times. At one point, they put together a meeting at CIA headquarters between Ames, a few other CIA officers, and a White House national security official just to keep him from going to Moscow. The topic of the meeting was CIA and SVR cooperation to combat the global drug trade. But now the clock was ticking.

Ames and his boss, Dave Edger, were scheduled to fly to Moscow on February 22, 1994.

Wiser believed it was time to arrest Ames and that the NIGHTMOVER team had built a strong case against him. But agents had never caught Ames in the act of stealing documents or exchanging money with the SVR. Direct evidence like that would have been a slam dunk in proving Ames was a Russian spy.

The FBI had instead gathered a mountain of circumstantial evidence. Wiser believed the facts of the case would show a jury that Rick Ames, aided by Rosario, had plotted to spy against the United States. Ames's betrayals had helped him make a killing.

Wiser had spent months writing details about the

evidence into an affidavit. That document, when completed, would run more than eleven thousand words. A federal judge would read it over before deciding whether the FBI had good cause to arrest Rick and Rosario Ames. Wiser hoped the judge would sign a warrant for the couple's arrest.

But what Wiser really wanted was a confession from Rick Ames. So he sought the advice of an expert in criminal behavior. One of the FBI's legendary profilers, Dick Ault, suggested that Wiser put on a bit of a show. The idea was to let Ames get a glimpse of all the work the NIGHTMOVER team had done to put him in handcuffs. These theatrics, Ault suggested, might prompt Ames to break down and confess to his crimes.

Wiser wasn't crazy about the idea, but he used it to come up with a plan.

CHAPTER 17

On President's Day 1994, the twenty-first day of February, Les Wiser woke at 3 A.M., showered, and put on a gray suit. Even though it was a federal holiday and the offices of the CIA and FBI were closed, he left his wife and two children and slipped behind the wheel of his 1991 Ford Taurus. Wiser reached the Buzzard Point field office hours before dawn, streetlights painting the gritty buildings an eerie orange. He parked in the office garage and made his way to the squad room.

At 6:30 A.M., the Gs radioed Wiser to let him know all was quiet at the Ames house. Wiser kept glancing at his watch. The face of the timepiece was stamped with the letters CCCP, the abbreviation for the USSR in Russian.

Wiser had bought the Soviet-made watch on a trip to Berlin. It was just before 7 A.M., the sun barely rising, when Wiser gave the order to move out.

The FBI put many dozens of employees on the streets that morning. By 7:30 A.M., most of the NIGHTMOVER team had gathered in the parking lot of a Roy Rogers restaurant in Tysons Corner, Virginia. (Today, the community calls itself Tysons.) Meanwhile, the Gs fanned out across Ames's Arlington neighborhood. A group of FBI agents took positions in the parking lot of a deli about four hundred yards from Ames's house.

At about 8 A.M., Wiser motored across a bridge spanning the Potomac River and made his way to the U.S. Attorney's office in Alexandria, Virginia. There, he met federal prosecutor Mark J. Hulkower. The two men walked into the office of U.S. Magistrate Judge Barry R. Poretz and presented him with Wiser's thick affidavit. The papers sought permission to arrest Rick and Rosario Ames. The agents also sought the judge's permission to search the couple's home and cars, Rick's office at the CIA, and a safe-deposit box at a local bank.

Poretz signed the papers at 9:55 A.M. Moments later,

Wiser climbed into a car with Hulkower and radioed the FBI command post in Tysons Corner.

"Okay," he said. "Go ahead."

Dave Edger phoned Ames from the Counternarcotics Center, reaching him at home at about 10 A.M.

"Rick," he said, "something important has just turned up." Edger explained that a cable had come in that had direct bearing on their trip to Moscow the following day. "You better come into the office. I think you need to see it now."

This was a trick, devised by Les Wiser, to get Ames out of his house.

Agents secretly listening to conversations in the Ames home heard Rick tell Rosario he had to go into the office. Moments later, Ames climbed into his Jaguar, leaving Rosario, Paul, and Rosario's mother at the house. As he motored through his quiet neighborhood, he lit up a cigarette and cracked the window of the Jag.

At that moment, Ames looked like any other affluent northern Virginian on a holiday Monday. He wore a dark green shirt, brown slacks, and loafers. His mustache was neatly trimmed. He might have been heading to the country club for a nice brunch. He eased the Jag up North Quebec Street, preparing to hang a right on Nellie Custis Drive. But ahead of him, he saw two cars side by side, brake lights glowing red.

He sat behind the autos for a moment, waiting for the car directly in front of him to make the turn and get out of his way. But then two other cars pulled up behind him. One drew so close that its grille came to rest inches from the rear bumper of the Jag.

There was no way Ames could have known that the driver of that car was Mike Donner, a brawny FBI agent who had spent months investigating him. Donner also happened to be a member of the FBI's elite SWAT team. He was trained for contacts with dangerous subjects, such as fugitives, killers, and kidnappers. Today, Donner's job was to prevent a high-speed chase of Ames in his Jag that would endanger innocent lives.

Donner set a red flashing light atop his dashboard. Ames, perhaps thinking he was in the way of an emergency vehicle, helpfully pulled his Jag closer to the concrete curb to let him pass. But Donner pulled his car forward, locking its front bumper against the Jaguar, pinning Ames in.

Donner and seven other agents popped out of four

cars, just as Les Wiser had choreographed. Dell Spry stalked up to Ames's window holding out his FBI credentials. He ordered Ames to keep his hands where he could see them. Ames, looking confused, hit a switch on the console of his car to lower the window.

"What?"

"Get out of the car," Donner shouted.

Ames opened the door and climbed to his feet, hastened by Donner's grip on his arm. Donner plucked the cigarette away from Ames, ordering him to put his hands on the car.

A team of FBI agents boxed in Rick Ames's Jaguar several blocks from his house on February 21, 1994, and arrested him on suspicion of espionage.

"You're under arrest, for espionage," Spry said, stepping behind Ames and pulling his arms behind him. He slapped handcuffs on each wrist and guided Ames, breathing hard, into the back seat of an FBI car. Rudy Guerin slid in next to him.

Ames had appeared shocked and frightened at first. Now he began to shout at the agents, telling them they were making a mistake.

"This is unbelievable," he said. *"Unbelievable!"*

"It's believable," Guerin said calmly. "And you better believe it."

Guerin hoped to strike a friendly tone with Ames. He spoke directly but politely, explaining that they were heading to the FBI office in Tysons Corner to talk. A talented interviewer, Guerin hoped to coax Ames into confessing to his crimes. If Ames agreed to speak to him, Guerin would continue to play the "good cop," the friendly ear willing to hear his side of the story. Donner, who had already demonstrated his gruff demeanor, would serve as the "bad cop," firing questions at him.

On the drive, perhaps trying to pull himself together, Ames whispered to himself:

"Think . . . think . . . think."

At about that time, the radio squawked.

"We have subject number two in custody, and we have the residence secured."

Ames crumpled forward in the back seat and, as Wiser recalled years later, "uttered a very naughty word."

CHAPTER 18

As the FBI was arresting Rick Ames, Special Agent Yolanda Larson had rung the doorbell at 2512 North Randolph Street. The Ameses' housekeeper opened the door to find two strangers on the stoop. Rosario, still in her bathrobe, moved down the stairs to greet Larson, who was pregnant and standing next to Agent John Hosinski.

The agents introduced themselves and asked Rosario to step outside. They didn't want five-year-old Paul Ames to hear what they were about to tell her. The agents explained to Rosario that Rick was under arrest for espionage, and so was she. They allowed her to go back into the house, change clothes, and wake her mother to explain what was happening. The agents instructed Rosario to take off her jewelry and leave her purse with them.

Rosario dressed and put on a camel hair coat. She hugged and kissed Paul and promised to be back soon. Agents helped the confused little boy fill his backpack with videos. His aunt, Rick Ames's sister, took him to her house.

Les Wiser's arrest operation had gone like clockwork. Agents took Rick and Rosario Ames into custody within minutes of each other. Wiser had wanted the agents to cuff them in different locations so the couple could not shout instructions to each other. Crime suspects, he knew, sometimes urged each other to clam up.

Wiser hoped both Ames and his wife would agree to speak to agents.

Not long after the arrests, Wiser walked into the Ames home for the very first time. The place was alive with agents and evidence techs. They were searching every inch of the house, bagging, tagging, and carting out evidence. Agents opened drawers and cabinets, looked under rugs, behind furniture, in the ceilings, anywhere Ames might have hidden records of his work for the KGB and SVR.

What they found was pure gold: a series of letters from Russian spies. Some of the notes dated back to Ames's CIA days in Rome, from 1986 to 1989. They learned that Ames had continued to meet with the KGB, handing over secrets for cold, hard cash. One of the letters uncovered by agents listed the names and addresses of all the dead drops and signal sites that Ames had used in the

D.C. metropolitan area. Perhaps the most eye-opening letter was from KGB agent Aleksei Khrenkov, who had served as one of Ames's handlers overseas.

"Dear Friend," it began. What followed was a calculation of all the money the KGB paid Ames from 1985 to May 1, 1989, a sum of nearly

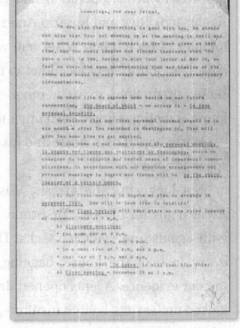

Russia's SVR spy service presented Ames with an accounting of the money he was paid for his betrayals of America from 1985 to 1989.

$2 million. "P.S.," the letter concluded, "We believe that these pictures would give You some idea about the beautiful piece of land on the river bank, which from now belongs to You forever. We decided not to take pictures of housing in this area with the understanding that You have much better idea of how Your country house (dacha) should look like. Good luck."

Wiser looked at the letter in amazement. It was a balance sheet for a spy—a gigantic brick to add to that wall of evidence. A very satisfying moment.

"He's toast," Wiser recalled thinking. "We got him."

But there was more.

Evidence techs picking through Ames's Jag found cassette tapes of jazz pianist Duke Ellington and classical music composer Vivaldi. But in the car's console they found evidence that was real music to their ears. It was no bigger than a lipstick case and had a value of about a quarter. It was a single stick of white chalk. Agents examined the chalk closely. They could see the tip of the stick had a blueish tint.

As if it had been drawn across a blue mailbox.

The arrest team brought Rick Ames to the FBI's satellite office in Tysons Corner, Virginia. There, the

NIGHTMOVER team had created a Hollywood version of a busy squad room. Domino's pizza boxes and cups of cold coffee littered the desks. Mounted on the walls and resting on easels were aerial images of the Ames home, dead drops, and surveillance images of Rick and Rosario. One enlarged image showed a chalk mark drawn on a blue mailbox, which agents were certain was the Smile signal site. Agents had stacked boxes in a corner that read "AMES." Agents had also set up a huge chart, created by the FBI crime lab. It read "AMES: ESPIONAGE."

The makeshift squad room was a complete fake. The photos, file boxes, coffee cups, and chart were just props. Wiser had wanted Ames to take one long look and come to grips with his situation: his goose was cooked. Wiser's great hope was that Ames would immediately confess to all his crimes.

Agents gave Ames a few moments to take in all the imagery. But he wouldn't give them the satisfaction. He scarcely glanced at his surroundings. Agents moved him into an interview room, where Guerin began a little speech he had practiced for months. He began by telling Ames that the FBI knew all about his espionage—the travels, the meetings, the money.

"What we really don't know," Guerin said, "is why."

In Guerin's hand was a paper that agents carry into meetings with people under arrest. It's called an advisement of rights form. Those who sign the form give up their legal rights to have a lawyer present during the interview. Guerin asked Ames if he would sign the paper, which he placed in front of his subject.

Ames slid the paper back to him.

"You can ask me questions," he told Guerin. "I just won't answer them."

Instead, Ames asked to speak with a lawyer.

Now, if Guerin had been an actor playing an FBI agent on TV, he would have slammed his fist on the table and cursed at Ames. He would have shouted that he wanted answers, and he wanted them right then. But in the real world of the FBI, the moment a subject says he wants a lawyer, the conversation ends. The men and women of the bureau are trained to treat that as if it were sacred.

Agents put Ames in a car and drove him to nearby Alexandria, Virginia, where he was fingerprinted, photographed, and booked into jail.

Les Wiser and the NIGHTMOVER team hoped the interrogation of Rosario Ames would go better. Agents had listened to more than two thousand hours of recorded conversations between Rick and Rosario. She had come off as a cold, arrogant, greedy wife. At one point in those secretly recorded chats, Rick Ames brought his wife breakfast in bed. How did she react? She browbeat him for bringing her runny eggs.

From what they had seen of Rick and Rosario's relationship, agents had a sense that she might sell Rick out to save herself from prison.

When Rosario sat down to talk with agents Yolanda Larson and John Hosinski, she said she knew nothing of Rick's espionage. She brought up the story Rick had told her, saying she thought the money had come from an old college buddy named Robert. Hosinski kept firing questions, poking holes in her story. But Rosario told them nothing about her role in Rick's espionage.

By late that afternoon, however, Rosario was worn down by the hammering of agents' questions. She finally broke down.

"Rick," she said, "works for the Russians."

A little before 5 P.M. that day, agents took Rosario Ames to the Alexandria Detention Center, the same jail where Rick was being held. She was fingerprinted and photographed and made to wear inmate clothing and sit with other felony suspects. There she lost it, screaming at her jailers.

Rick Ames heard the clamor from his cell and began to weep. Years later, he would describe his anguish to author Pete Earley.

"I kept thinking, 'How could I have been so dumb that I didn't see this coming?' In retrospect, there were so many signals. I kept going over and over in my mind what I should have done. The only thing that kept me from killing myself was that I kept thinking, 'No, you gotta help Rosario and Paul. Then you can kill yourself, but not now, not yet.'"

At CIA headquarters that day, Sandy Grimes, Paul Redmond, and Jeanne Vertefeuille cheered the news of Ames's arrest. Someone had brought a bottle of champagne to toast the happy occasion. But they were so wrung out that, even in their triumph over Ames, they forgot to drink it.

EPILOGUE

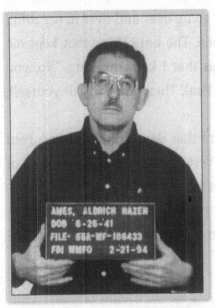

Aldrich H. "Rick" Ames was booked into the Alexandria Detention Center on February 21, 1994, shortly after his arrest for espionage.

Rick Ames faced a potential punishment of life in prison for what he would later describe as the "mistaken and catastrophic choices" he made between 1985 and the day of his arrest. Ames's court-appointed lawyer, who had defended other spies, urged Ames to take his case before a jury.

But Ames refused. He had betrayed his country, sent ten spies to their deaths, and ruined his life. Now he wanted to do what he could to make things right for his son, Paul.

On the final Thursday in April 1994, Rick and Rosario Ames appeared before U.S. District Judge Claude M. Hilton in the U.S. District Court in Alexandria. Both pleaded guilty to their plot to commit espionage and to tax fraud. Paul was already in Bogotá, living with Rosario's family.

Prosecutor Mark Hulkower told the court that Ames had caused the deaths of U.S. assets just as surely as if he had pulled the trigger himself. And why? "Because Rick Ames wasn't making enough money [at] the CIA," he said, "and wanted to live in a half-million-dollar house and drive a Jaguar."

Now, Hulkower told the judge, it was time for Ames to pay the price.

Ames addressed the courtroom as Rosario, clutching a crucifix, sobbed uncontrollably. "I bitterly regret the catastrophe which my betrayal of trust brought upon my wife and son and upon any who have loved or cared for me," he said. He did not apologize to the CIA, or to the Russian spies who had lost their lives because of him.

Judge Hilton pronounced Ames and Rosario guilty of their plot to commit espionage. He sentenced Ames to serve the rest of his life in prison with no chance of parole. But before imposing a sentence on Rosario, he required that Ames meet with FBI agents and CIA officers and tell them everything he had done during his nine years as a Russian spy. The judge said he would sentence Rosario after those debriefings.

Jeanne Vertefeuille took part in the first of Ames's many debriefings. She was joined by FBI agents Les Wiser, Mike Donner, Rudy Guerin, and Jim Milburn. That meeting took place in a conference room at the FBI office in Tysons Corner. There, Vertefeuille heard a most chilling story.

Ames told his debriefers that KGB officers, working hard to prevent him from getting caught, had asked him for the names of anyone in the CIA who could be blamed for his own crimes. They wanted to frame one of his colleagues, someone also familiar with the Soviet agents he had betrayed.

"You're not going to like this," Ames said, shooting a look at Vertefeuille, "but I gave them your name."

Vertefeuille was stunned. A brother officer had given her name to the KGB, the CIA's greatest enemy, in hopes she would be prosecuted for his crimes.

Vertefeuille, a CIA legend who paved the way for generations of women to become officers in the agency, would die of a malignant brain tumor in January 2013.

Sandy Grimes, whose work at the CIA played a key role in unmasking Ames as a Russian spy, co-wrote a book with her good friend Jeanne Vertefeuille that was published after Vertefeuille's death. The book, *Circle of Treason: A CIA Account of Traitor Aldrich Ames and the Men He Betrayed*, offers an inside account of their mole hunt.

Grimes cannot forgive Ames for his betrayals, which caused the deaths of two brave Soviet spies she had sworn to protect.

"The only thing he had to sell," she said, "was human lives."

Rosario Ames returned to court on October 21, 1994. Wearing a green jail uniform, she stood before Judge Hilton and described her husband to the court as a master liar and manipulator. Those traits made him a good intelligence officer, she said, but a "deadly tool in the hands of the Russians." She asked the judge for leniency so she could get back to raising her son.

"I beg you, your honor, Paul needs me," she said.

"Paul is innocent. He did nothing wrong."

The judge was unmoved. He sentenced Rosario to five years and three months in prison. When she had completed her time behind bars, the U.S. government deported her to her native Colombia, where she reunited with her son.

Rick Ames today is inmate number 40087-083 in a federal prison in Terre Haute, Indiana. He turned seventy-eight years old in May 2019.

Rosario Ames was booked into jail just a few blocks from the courthouse where she and her husband faced trial for their plot to sell classified files to Russian spies.

Les Wiser Jr. remains fiercely proud of the FBI's work in bringing Ames to justice. He still thinks about the brave spies who died in service to the United States because Ames betrayed them.

"Those people were a safety valve for peace," Wiser said. "[Ames] made it a more dangerous world."

In 1995, a year after the NIGHTMOVER team arrested Ames, the director of the CIA awarded Wiser the National Intelligence Medal of Achievement for his work managing the Ames investigation. The Soviet-made watch that Wiser wore during the case is merely a memento today. "Just like everything else in the Soviet Union," he said, "it quit working."

Les Wiser appeared in court during hearings for Rick and Rosario Ames, where a courtroom sketch artist captured his image on the witness stand. Federal courts in the United States prohibit cameras.

Wiser retired from the FBI as special agent in charge of the New Jersey field office in 2007. He spent the next year serving as director of security for the Prudential Center, home of the New Jersey Devils professional hockey team. Today Wiser is an instructor at the University of South Carolina in Columbia, where he teaches criminal justice and serves as director of internships.

He cherishes his family time.

Author's Note

Everyone loves a good spy story.

The tale of turncoat CIA officer Aldrich "Rick" Ames is one of the all-time best. There are many books published on the Ames case, but the one you just read is the first written exclusively for young readers.

The timing of this book, with its rich cast of Russian spies, couldn't be better. As I write these very words, America's news reports are dominated by stories of Russian spies who waged a secret campaign to undermine the 2016 presidential election.

True spy stories are hard to tell because certain parts of the tale remain secret. For instance, neither the FBI nor the CIA will name the Russian source who helped pinpoint Rick Ames as the deadly traitor. But many of the files in the Ames case are public.

To research *Catching a Russian Spy*, I read thousands of pages about the life and crimes of Rick Ames. This included six books on the Ames case, mounds of court records, news stories, and long interviews with Ames and others. I also reviewed print, video, and radio interviews with key participants in the story.

After this research, I conducted long interviews with two of the main characters in the story, former FBI agent Leslie G. "Les" Wiser Jr. and former CIA officer Sandy Grimes. I also renewed my correspondence with Ames, with whom I had traded letters during my research for another book I wrote called *The Spy's Son*. Then I created a color-coded timeline on an Excel spreadsheet. This chronology, which spans hundreds of pages, begins with Ames's birth in 1941 and ends in 1994, the year of his arrest.

I have written this book as if I were writing a novel. But unlike a novel, all the words you just read are true.

THE WALL OF
HONOR

A wall on the top floor of FBI headquarters is devoted to the men and women of the bureau who gave their lives protecting the United States. Smaller memorials adorn the walls of FBI field offices across the nation.

The Wall of Honor today honors thirty-six agents known as "Service Martyrs," who died in direct conflict with wrongdoers. They are joined by more than forty other FBI workers killed on the job.

Former Special Agent Mike Anderson, who played a role in the espionage investigation of Aldrich Hazen "Rick" Ames, knows the sacrifices of the honorees.

His own father's face is on the wall.

Special Agent Terry Ray Anderson, Mike's dad, was shot to death on May 17, 1966, while taking part in a massive manhunt. Seventeen-year-old Peggy Ann Bradnick had been kidnapped by William Hollenbaugh and taken to a remote section of the Appalachian Mountains. While searching near Shade Gap, Pennsylvania, Anderson spotted a dog that belonged to Hollenbaugh. He bravely followed the animal as it trotted back to its owner. But Hollenbaugh ambushed Anderson, shooting him with a handgun. Bradnick watched in horror as Anderson took his last breath. A day later, as more than 1,000 searchers took part in what was then the biggest manhunt in U.S. history, a state trooper shot and killed Hollenbaugh.

Bradnick would never forget the FBI agent who died trying to save her.

"He sacrificed his life for me," Bradnick told a reporter during a 2011 memorial for Anderson. "I'll never forget him." Terry Anderson became the fifteenth agent honored by the FBI as a Service Martyr.

Mike Anderson was twelve years old when his father was killed. Like his dad, he served a distinguished career in the FBI.

The first name put on the Wall of Honor was Special Agent Edwin C. Shanahan, a kind-eyed man with slicked-back hair murdered in a 1925 shootout with a car thief in Chicago. The FBI tracked his killer to Texas. Later, they found him on a train near St. Louis, Missouri, where agents pounced on him before he could grab the guns he carried in his luggage and overcoat.

The wall also honors more than forty other FBI agents and personnel who died while performing law enforcement duties. More than a dozen of those men and women rushed to the scenes of jetliner crashes on 9/11, where jet fuel and smoldering debris burned for days. They inhaled toxic fumes and handled contaminated soil that exposed them to cancers that later took their lives, earning them places on the wall.

ALDRICH AMES TIMELINE

May 26, 1941: Aldrich Hazen Ames is born in River Falls, Wisconsin.

1952: Carleton Ames, Rick's father, joins the CIA. He first serves overseas, then moves his family to McLean, Virginia, near agency headquarters.

1959–1962: Rick Ames graduates from McLean High School and begins college in Chicago, but flunks out. He moves back home and becomes a full-time clerk typist for the CIA.

1967–1968: Ames graduates from George Washington University. The CIA accepts him into its junior training program. He completes "spy school."

May 24, 1969: Ames marries Nancy Jane Segebarth, a fellow CIA officer.

1969–1972: The CIA assigns Ames and his wife to Ankara, Turkey. There, they pose as civilian workers at a military base. Ames is supposed to recruit Soviet agents, but he fails. His boss gives him a poor job evaluation.

1972: Ames is reassigned to CIA headquarters to learn the Russian language.

Mid-1970s: Ames gets a big break—he serves as handler for a Soviet diplomat. The CIA equips this agent with a spy camera disguised as a tube of lip balm. The KGB later arrests the agent. Fearing torture, he swallows a CIA-issued suicide pill and dies.

1976–1981: Ames is assigned to the CIA's office in New York. He poses as Andy Robinson, a business tycoon. He soon is handler for two major Soviet spies. One is the ambassador to the United Nations. Ames's star is on the rise.

Fall 1981: Ames transfers from New York to Mexico City. He now poses as a U.S. Foreign Service officer. He runs the CIA station's Soviet counterintelligence (CI) branch. His wife Nancy, who has left the CIA, remains in New York.

Summer 1982: In Mexico City, Ames meets Maria del Rosario Casas Dupuy, of Bogotá. She works in the Colombian embassy. They begin a torrid love affair.

1983: Ames is reassigned to CIA headquarters as a branch chief in the Soviet/East European Division. Although still married to Nancy, he proposes to Rosario. They take an apartment together near his work.

Late 1984: Ames and his wife Nancy settle their divorce. He is thousands of dollars in debt. Starting in June 1985, he must pay her $300 a month in spousal support.

April 1985: Ames, about to turn forty-four, decides to switch teams to make money. He plots to sell some CIA files to the KGB.

April 16, 1985: Ames leaves a note for the KGB at the Soviet embassy in Washington. He asks for $50,000 in exchange for information on Soviets the CIA hopes to recruit.

May 1985: Ames returns to the Soviet embassy, where he meets KGB officer Victor Cherkashin, the CI chief in Washington. Cherkashin lets Ames know the KGB accepts his offer. Ames later receives $50,000.

June 13, 1985: Ames passes a plastic bag full of files to the KGB. It holds the names, or code names, of dozens of KGB and Soviet bloc spies secretly working for the CIA. Investigators later call this betrayal "the big dump."

August 10, 1985: Ames marries Rosario, now a U.S. citizen, in a small wedding in Virginia.

Fall 1985: KGB officers betrayed by Ames begin to vanish. Some are arrested. Inside the CIA, the news is met with panic. Over the next few years, the agency learns that all of its Soviet and Eastern European agents were compromised. Ten have been executed.

1986: Ames is reassigned to Rome, where he continues to meet with Soviet handlers. He turns over classified reports—about a thousand a year—in exchange for bricks of $100 bills.

1986–1989: Back at CIA headquarters, teams of investigators try to learn who gave up the names of the Soviet assets. They have no clue that the culprit is in Rome, driving an Alfa Romeo sports car, dressing like a movie star, and stashing money in Swiss bank accounts.

November 11, 1988: Paul Ames is born in Rome. He will be Rick and Rosario's only child.

June 1989: Ames receives a letter from his KGB masters in Rome. It's an accounting of his pay. So far, he has received nearly $1.9 million, with promises of more. (The Soviets would eventually pay or set aside $4.6 million for Ames.)

1989 to 1993: Ames and his family return to Washington, D.C. His new position at CIA headquarters gives him access to more files that are valuable to the KGB. His Soviet handlers set up dead drops where he hides those files in and around Washington. The KGB meets him in different spots around the world, paying him in bricks of $100 bills.

1993: A team of mole hunters in the CIA discover that Ames has paid cash for a $540,000 home in Arlington, Virginia (valued today at $1 million). The team secretly examines his CIA assignments and bank records. They find that he has made huge cash deposits after meetings with a Soviet diplomat.

May 1993: The FBI opens an espionage investigation against Ames. The probe later reveals that Rosario is in on his plot.

February 21, 1994: The FBI arrests Ames and his wife, accusing them of plotting to commit espionage and hiding $2.5 million in proceeds from the Internal Revenue Service.

April 28, 1994: Rick and Rosario Ames plead guilty to their crimes. Rick Ames agrees to serve a life prison sentence with no possibility of parole in exchange for leniency for Rosario. A judge later sentences her to a little more than five years in prison.

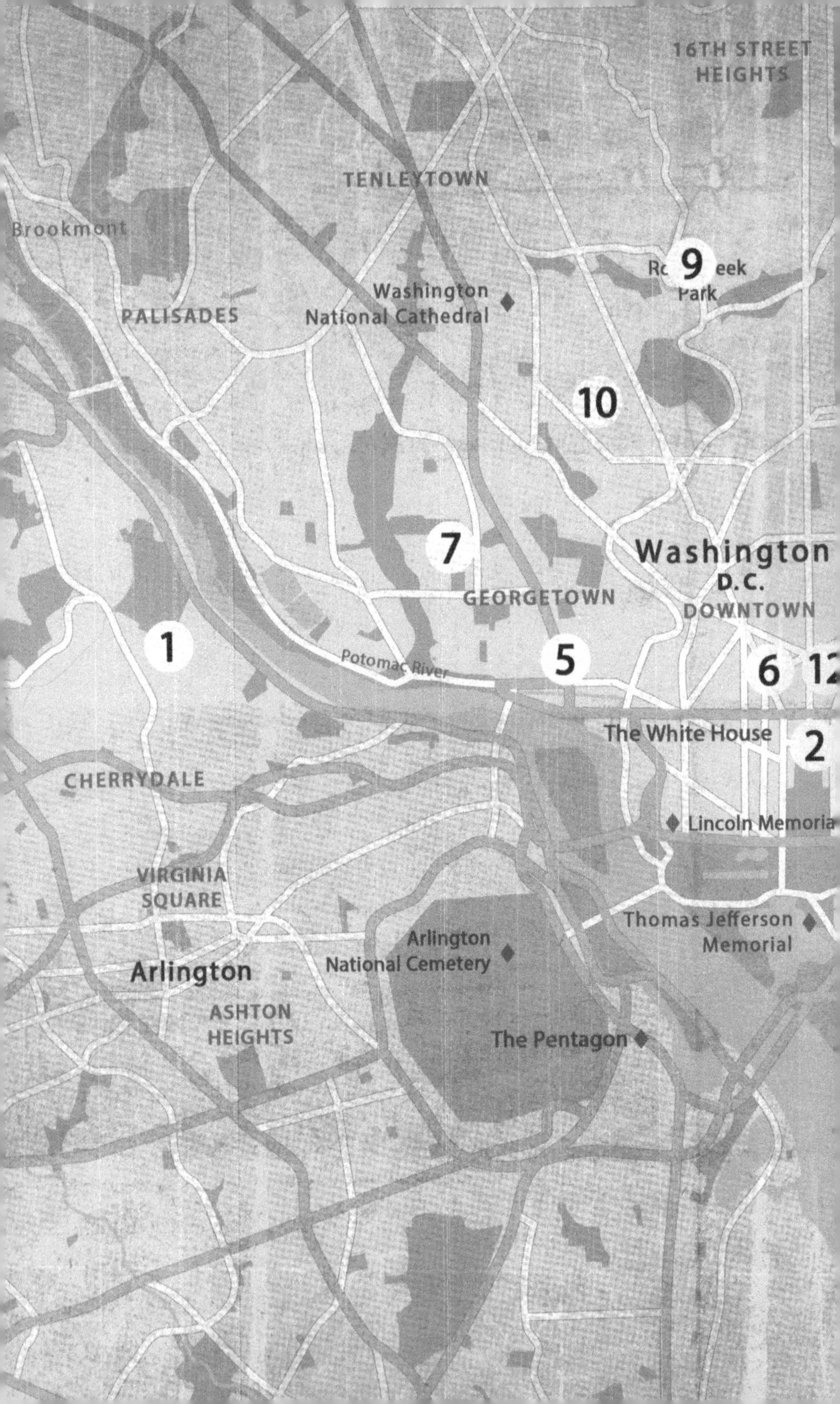
16TH STREET HEIGHTS
TENLEYTOWN
Brookmont
Rock Creek Park
Washington National Cathedral
PALISADES
10
7
Washington
D.C.
GEORGETOWN
DOWNTOWN
1
Potomac River
5
6
12
The White House
2
CHERRYDALE
Lincoln Memorial
VIRGINIA SQUARE
Thomas Jefferson Memorial
Arlington National Cemetery
Arlington
ASHTON HEIGHTS
The Pentagon
9

(1) Ames home: 2512 North Randolph St., Arlington, VA

(2) White House, 1600 Pennsylvania Ave.

(3) U.S. Department of Justice, 950 Pennsylvania Ave.

(4) FBI Headquarters, 935 Pennsylvania Ave.

(5) Chadwicks Restaurant, 3205 K Street NW

(6) Mayflower Hotel, 1127 Connecticut Ave. NW

(7) Smile signal site, 37th and R

(8) CIA headquarters

(9) Bridge dead drop

(10) Rose signal site

(11) FBI Washington Metropolitan Field Office

(12) Embassy of the Soviet Union

A Glossary of Spy Terms

agent: a person who secretly obtains information for an intelligence service such as the CIA

asset: any person or device that aids a spy operation

beacon (or tracker): a device typically hidden in a vehicle that allows agents to track its movements. They used to work on radio frequencies, but today they use GPS technology.

black bag job (also known as a sneak and peek): any secret entry into a home or auto (often by picking a lock) to collect clues or evidence. The FBI conducts such operations with court approval.

blown cover: when a spy's true identity is exposed

bug: a tiny, hidden device that allows spies to listen in on conversations

cable: a secret report passed to CIA stations all over the world

CIA: the Central Intelligence Agency, founded in 1947,

is America's best-known spy service. The CIA's spies, known as intelligence officers, are stationed all over the world. They collect information, often from contacts they meet overseas. But unlike the FBI, they have no law-enforcement functions.

code name: a name given by the CIA or another intelligence service to an agent or an investigation

counterespionage: the protection of secret materials from foreign spies

counterintelligence (CI): measures taken to prevent spying or sabotage by foreign spies

cover: a false identity taken by a spy

dead drop: a hiding spot shared by two spies so they are not seen together. Each visits the site alone to exchange money, secrets, or plans.

espionage: the work of professional spies, also called intelligence gathering

Farm, the: the CIA's covert training center

FBI: the Federal Bureau of Investigation, founded in 1908, is the leading security and intelligence-gathering service in the U.S. homeland

FISA: the Foreign Intelligence Surveillance Act of 1978 created a secretive court based in Washington, D.C., whose judges sign orders that allow the

FBI to eavesdrop on suspected foreign spies and terrorists

GRU: the spy service for Russia's military

handlers (also known as controls): intelligence officers who direct and pay foreign agents to spy for them

intelligence officer: the preferred title for professional spies working for the CIA and other intelligence services around the world

JOYRIDE: the CIA's code name for the Aldrich Ames investigation

KGB: the Soviet Union's primary security and spy service from its founding in 1954 until the USSR's collapse in 1991

mole: an intelligence officer secretly working for another spy service. A mole obtains secrets on the job and provides them to the other nation.

NIGHTMOVER: the FBI's code name for the Aldrich Ames investigation

pole camera: a camera secretly placed on a fixed object, such as a telephone pole, to capture images of people and places under investigation

Russian Federation: Moscow is the capital of this nation formed after the collapse of the Soviet Union. Russia stretches to eleven time zones—from Western Europe to the Bering Strait off Alaska.

safe house: a secure house, apartment, or hotel suite from which a spy service runs covert operations

signal site: a spot where agents and their handlers signal plans to each other

Soviet Union: Moscow was the capital of this superpower, which existed from 1922 to 1991. Its formal name in English was the Union of Soviet Socialist Republics (USSR).

SVR: Russia's foreign intelligence service

tap/wiretapping: the secret monitoring of telephone or Internet conversations

tradecraft: the art and craft of espionage, sometimes called spycraft

walk-in: a person who volunteers to spy for a foreign government

ACKNOWLEDGMENTS

I am indebted, as always, to the men and women of the FBI—past and present—for their help and guidance in the FBI Files series. Special thanks go to Christopher Allen and Shelley Wilson in the Investigative Publicity and Public Affairs Unit at FBI headquarters.

My warmest thanks to former FBI supervisor Leslie G. "Les" Wiser Jr., the hero of this book, whose insights, recollections, and wonderfully dry humor made my work so much fun. Many thanks also to former CIA officer Sandy Grimes, another heroic figure in this story and one of the coolest characters I've ever met.

A special shout-out to three exceptional women: To Kristin Margaret Graeper Quinlan, my partner in crime, who during the writing of this book agreed to marry me. To Tamar Rydzinski, my agent and founder of Context Literary Agency, who always knows the best doors to open for me. And to Katherine Jacobs, my very talented editor, who, in concert with her unsung colleagues at Roaring Brook Press, produces amazing books.

I am grateful for the groundbreaking work performed by the following authors whose books chronicled the Aldrich Ames spy case: James Adams, Pete Earley, Sandra Grimes, David Johnston, Neil A. Lewis, Peter Maas, Jeanne Vertefeuille, Tim Weiner, and especially David Wise, the dean of American spy writers, who died in 2018.

A tip of the hat also to the great journalists who covered developments in the Ames spy case as it unfolded. This book is a reflection of their best work.

It is fitting that I close by thanking my fellow American journalists, whose daily reports serve as the first draft of history. You face layoffs and crippling wage cuts, and a staggering number of you die on dangerous assignments around the world. You hammer away only to hear people in power foolishly call you enemies of the American people. You remind me of the introduction to the old Superman TV show: "And who, disguised as Clark Kent, mild-mannered reporter for a great metropolitan newspaper, fights a never-ending battle for truth, justice, and the American way." Godspeed, my friends. Make that first draft of history sing.

Sources

Books

Adams, James. *Sellout: Aldrich Ames and the Corruption of the CIA.* New York: Viking, 1995.

Earley, Pete. *Confessions of a Spy: The Real Story of Aldrich Ames.* New York: Putnam, 1997.

Grimes, Sandra, and Jeanne Vertefeuille. *Circle of Treason: A CIA Account of Traitor Aldrich Ames and the Men He Betrayed.* Annapolis, MD: Naval Institute Press, 2012.

Maas, Peter. *Killer Spy: The Inside Story of the FBI's Pursuit and Capture of Aldrich Ames, America's Deadliest Spy.* New York: Warner Books, 1995.

Weiner, Tim, David Johnston, and Neil A. Lewis. *Betrayal: The Story of Aldrich Ames, an American Spy.* New York: Random House, 1995.

Wise, David. *Nightmover: How Aldrich Ames Sold the CIA to the KGB for $4.6 Million.* New York: HarperCollins, 1995.

U.S. Government Reports

Aldrich Ames Criminal Complaint, U.S. District Court, Eastern District of Virginia, February 22, 1994.

Ames IRS Petition: Aldrich H. Ames, Petitioner v. Commissioner of Internal Revenue, Respondent, May 28, 1999. www.leagle.com/decision /1999416112ttc3041397.

Central Intelligence Agency. *The People of the CIA . . . Ames Mole Hunt Team*. March 12, 2009. www.cia .gov/news-information/featured-story-archive/ames -mole-hunt-team.html.

Deutch, John. *Statement of the Director of Central Intelligence on the Clandestine Services and the Damage Caused by Aldrich Ames*. December 7, 1995.

Hitz, Frederick P. *Statement of Frederick P. Hitz, Inspector General, Central Intelligence Agency, on the Ames Investigation*. Permanent Select Committee on Intelligence, United States House of Representatives, and the Select Committee on Intelligence, United States Senate. September 28, 1994.

Permanent Select Committee on Intelligence, U.S. House of Representatives. *Report of Investigation:*

The Aldrich Ames Espionage Case. November 30, 1994.

U.S. Department of Justice, Office of the Inspector General. *A Review of the FBI's Performance in Uncovering the Espionage Activities of Aldrich Hazen Ames*. U.S. Department of Justice/Office of the Inspector General Special Report Unclassified Executive Summary. April 1997. https://oig.justice.gov/special/9704.htm.

U.S. Senate Select Committee on Intelligence. *Interview with Aldrich Ames*. August 5, 1994.

U.S. Senate Select Committee on Intelligence. *An Assessment of the Aldrich H. Ames Espionage Case and Its Implications for U.S. Intelligence*. November 1, 1994. www.intelligence.senate.gov/sites/default/files/publications/10390.pdf.

News Broadcasts and Published Interviews

"Aldrich Ames CIA Traitor." *Witness History*. BBC World, February 23, 2015. www.bbc.co.uk/programmes/p02k55xf.

"Interview with Sandy Grimes." Episode 21: Spies. National Security Archive, January 30, 1998.

https://nsarchive2.gwu.edu/coldwar/interviews
/episode-21/grimes1.html.

"Rationalizing Treason: An Interview with Aldrich
Ames." CNN Cold War series, 1998.

Shannon, Elaine. "Death of the Perfect Spy." *Time*,
June 24, 2001. http://content.time.com/time
/magazine/article/0,9171,164863,00.html.

Wynkoop, Susan. "Interview of Former Special
Agent of the FBI Marvin O'Dell Spry." Society
of Former Special Agents of the FBI, October 15,
2009. www.discoveryvirginia.org/islandora/object
/islandora%3A12296.

Newspaper Articles

Isikoff, Michael. "CIA Creates Narcotics Unit to Help in
Drug Fight." *The Washington Post*, May 28, 1989.

Jackson, Robert L., and Ronald J. Ostrow. "Wife of CIA
Double Agent Sentenced to 5 Years in Prison." *Los
Angeles Times*, October 22, 1994.

Johnston, David. "How the F.B.I. Finally Caught Aldrich
Ames." *The New York Times*, January 27, 1995.

Johnston, David. "Prosecutors Say Official at C.I.A. Spied
for Russia." *The New York Times*, February 23, 1994.

Martin, Douglas. "Jeanne Vertefeuille, C.I.A. Official Who Helped Catch a Notorious Mole, Dies at 80." *The New York Times*, January 11, 2013.

Martin, John. "Spy-Catcher to Head FBI's Newark Office." *The Star-Ledger* (Newark, NJ), May 5, 2005.

Miller, Bill, and Walter Pincus. "Ames Pleads Guilty to Spying, Gets Life Term." *The Washington Post*, April 29, 1994.

Pincus, Walter. "Ames Met Two Russians in the '70s, and Therein Lies a Tale of Deceit." *The Washington Post*, April 27, 1994.

Pincus, Walter. "Naming Those Betrayed by Ames." *The Washington Post*, June 12, 1995.

Quinn, Sally. "The Terrible Secret of Rosario Ames." *The Washington Post*, October 19, 1994.

Weiner, Tim. "Why I Spied; Aldrich Ames." *The New York Times Magazine*, July 31, 1994.

Photo credits

PHOTO CREDITS

Page 3: Federal Bureau of Investigation (FBI), United States Department of Justice; 30: Central Intelligence Agency (CIA); 32: Central Intelligence Agency (CIA); 72: Federal Bureau of Investigation (FBI), United States Department of Justice; 89: Federal Bureau of Investigation (FBI), United States Department of Justice; 92: Federal Bureau of Investigation (FBI), United States Department of Justice; 110: Federal Bureau of Investigation (FBI), United States Department of Justice; 112: Federal Bureau of Investigation (FBI), United States Department of Justice; 116: Federal Bureau of Investigation (FBI), United States Department of Justice; 122: Federal Bureau of Investigation (FBI), United States Department of Justice; 159: Bryan Denton.